FROM
SPANIARD
TO CREOLE

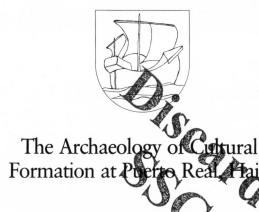

The Archaeology of Cultural
Formation at Puerto Real, Haiti

Charles R. Ewen

The University of Alabama Press
Tuscaloosa and London

The paper on which this book is printed meets the minimum requirements of
American National Standard for Information Science-Permanence of Paper for
Printed Library Materials, ANSI A39.48–1984.

Library of Congress Cataloging-in-Publication Data

Ewen, Charles Robin.
   From Spaniard to Creole : the archaeology of
cultural formation at Puerto Real, Haiti / by Charles Robin Ewen.
      p.   cm.
   Includes bibliographical references and index.
   ISBN 0-8173-0498-3
   1. Puerto Real Site (Haiti) 2. Haiti—Antiquities. 3. Haiti—
History—To 1791. 4. Spaniards—Colonization—Haiti—History—16th
century. 5. Spain—Colonies—America—History—16th century.
6. Excavations (Archaeology)—Haiti. I. Title.
F1911.E94   1991
972.94—dc20   90-40044

British Library Cataloging-in-Publication Data available

To the Haitian people
of Limonade and En Bas Saline
for their indulgence, hard work, and good humor.

Contents

Illustrations

Tables

Acknowledgments

The initial work at Puerto Real for this project was facilitated by the Institute de Sauvegarde du Patrimoine National (ISPAN), under the direction of M. Albert Mangones. Later, the Institute National Haitien de la Culture et des Artes (INAHCA) assumed the role of primary sponsor, and Dr. Max Paul of the Bureau d'Ethnologie aided our efforts. Funding for the project was provided by the Organization of American States, represented in Haiti by M. Ragnar Arnessen; and by a grant from the National Endowment for the Humanities (RO-20935-85), awarded to the University of Florida Center for Early Contact Period Studies with Dr. Kathleen Deagan as principal investigator.

While at the University of Florida, I received assistance from a variety of sources. A University of Florida, Division of Sponsored Research, graduate-school fellowship was followed by a teaching assistantship with the Department of Anthropology. The final preparation of my dissertation was supported by the College of Liberal Arts and Sciences and the Center for Early Contact Period Studies. Its help interspersed throughout, the Florida State Museum also provided facilities and part-time employment when they were needed.

Faunal analysis and production of this work were completed with the help of a Charles H. Fairbanks Award from the Department of Anthropology at the University of Florida.

The preparation of the manuscript took place in Tallahassee and Fayetteville, Arkansas. During my time in Tallahassee, Jim Miller, Dr. John Scarry, Dr. Bonnie McEwan, and Dr. Jeffrey Mitchem gave me valuable advice that both directly and indirectly assisted in editing the manuscript. The final version was completed in Fayetteville, where I was able to impose upon the staff and facilities of the Arkansas Archeological Survey. I am also grateful for the patience of Robert Ferris, manuscript editor for The University of Alabama Press, who diplomatically suggested felicitous editorial changes without altering my ideas or intentions in any way or damaging the fragile ego associated with a first book.

Many faculty members guided my research, and to them I am greatly indebted: first and foremost, my dissertation committee chair, Dr. Kathleen Deagan. She brought intellectual and professional order to an otherwise too-casual graduate student and helped to impart the academic, administrative, and political skills necessary to cope with the post-student world. The other members of my committee were Dr. Jerald Milanich, Dr. Elizabeth Wing, Dr. Lyle McAlister, and Dr. Michael Gannon, who were all available when I needed them. Dr. Gannon deserves special thanks for "being there" when my funds ran out at the Grand Hotel Oloffson in Port-au-Prince. Dr. David Geggus could not "be there" at the end, but he did help me start off on the right foot.

Although the actual writing was a solitary task, performed in various locations in Gainesville, Tallahassee, and Fayetteville, the recovery and analysis of the data involved a multitude of people, to whom I am most grateful. In the field, assistance at the site was ably given by Greg Smith and Patti Peacher. Greg also helped keep me sane both in the field and during the preparation of the dissertation. In the field lab, Tim Deagan and Jim Cusick somehow kept up with a daily torrent of artifacts. Maurice Williams shared his experiences at and knowledge of the site.

I am especially indebted to Dr. William Hodges, of the Hopital le Bon Samaritan, for discovering the site and forcing me to justify my interpretations on the occasions when they differed from his own. Most of the fieldwork was done by local Haitian villagers. These men formed the best field crew I have ever had the privilege to work with. They were extremely patient with my Creole, were always in good humor, and were true artists with a trowel. Gratitude is also extended to the Haitian students who came up from Port-au-Prince to work on the project.

Back in the United States, Greg Smith, Bonnie McEwan, and John Marron aided with the analysis. John is to be commended for completing the tedious task of coding and entering the data; let it be noted that this was *not* a thankless task. The excellent artifact photographs were taken by James Quine and serve to accentuate my own shortcomings in field photography. Charles Poe drafted two of the illustrations. The faunal analysis was performed under the direction of Dr. Elizabeth Wing in the Florida State Museum Zoo-archaeology Laboratory, by Karen Walker, Susan DeFrance, and Karla Bosworth, who had been involved with that exacting task in a previous project. I deeply appreciate their efforts. I am also very grateful to Dr. Ray Willis, Dr. Rochelle Marrinan, Jennifer Hamilton, Dr. Bonnie McEwan, the late Dr. Gary Shapiro, and Alicia Kemper. Their work preceded mine and I benefited from it.

The manuscript was improved by the comments of Stanley South, Dr. Jeffrey Brain, and Dr. Marvin Smith. I am especially indebted to Marvin for analyzing the beads collected from Puerto Real and for insisting that the artifacts be more adequately described. Judith Knight is most responsible for my dissertation being transformed into a book. Her comments and encouragement from the book rooms at various conferences provided the necessary incentive to rewrite my dissertation at a point when I thought I could no longer bear to look at it.

The final round of applause goes to those who less formally, though no less importantly, contributed to the completion of this volume. Charles Poe, Richard Vernon, Lee Nabergall, and Rich and Barbara Johnson helped me recover from a car accident in Tallahassee, enabling me to continue to write. Jeff Brautigam tolerated my near takeover of our office in Gainesville and listened politely to the reading of rough drafts. My good friend Russ Skowronek commiserated with me and spurred my progress in a spirit of friendly competition. Kathy Gladden typed portions of the manuscript and provided an atmosphere of order and support. Finally my family—

Rob, Maggie, and Meg Ewen—have stood by me throughout my many years in school. Although chiding me to work harder, they were always proud of the results. Thank you.

This book is truly the result of the work of many individuals. However, I assume full responsibility for any errors or omissions.

Charles R. Ewen

FROM
SPANIARD
TO CREOLE

1

Introduction

Puerto Real, founded in 1503 just over a decade after Columbus's initial voyage of discovery, was one of the earliest Spanish colonial settlements in the New World. The site provides an important opportunity for archaeological research into initial Spanish colonial adaptations and their role in the development of a Hispanic-American colonial tradition. This research makes it possible to identify specific ways in which sixteenth-century Iberian colonists adapted to the new social, economic, and environmental conditions. Through the combination and exchange of Old World and New World cultural and physical elements, the colonists created an adaptive tradition that characterized the pioneer Spanish settlements and represented the earliest expression of Hispanic-American culture.

The approach to the study of culture contact and acculturation taken in this volume is somewhat unusual in that it emphasizes the effects of the New World inhabitants and environment on the European colonists. Traditional studies of acculturation have predominantly dealt with the impact of the colonial power on the indigenous peoples (Foster 1960:7). Researchers should not forget that the process was not a one-way transfer of traits (i.e., colonists to indigenous peoples), but rather an unequal exchange. The Spaniards, though not suffering the enormous cultural transformations thrust upon the Indians, did experience significant social modifications. It is these modifications that this study will seek to elucidate.

This particular study of culture contact and change is confined to

Spanish colonial activity in the New World. It is expected that by examining Iberian adaptive responses in two settings (i.e., Puerto Real, Haiti, and St. Augustine, Florida) it will be possible to arrive at some generalizations concerning Spanish colonization strategies and how they are reflected in the archaeological record. It is important to build solid mid-range theory if archaeologists are ever to attempt to formulate general theories concerning human behavior.

Because of the observation of the Columbian quincentenary in 1992, scholarly as well as popular attention has been drawn to Spain's activities in the Western Hemisphere. Several historical, anthropological, and archaeological works (cf. Deagan 1983, Floyd 1973, Foster 1960, Gongora 1975, Sauer 1966) deal specifically with Spanish colonial adaptations to the New World. Of these, the works of Foster and Deagan have most directly influenced the author of this volume.

Foster (1960:7–12) provides the working theoretical model for this study with his idea of a "culture of conquest." He acknowledges that, in contact situations, the major changes are to be found in the culture of the recipient group. However, the donor group, or "conquest culture," also changes its character to some degree. Foster (1960:233) states that the basic colonial cultures took shape relatively rapidly. As they became more successful in satisfying the basic needs of the colonists, they become more static, or "crystallized" to use Foster's term. Once crystallized, the culture became more resistant to change from the mother country. It was predicted before the fieldwork that this situation would be manifest at Puerto Real.

The most extensive archaeological study of Spanish colonial adaptation to the New World to date has been conducted in St. Augustine, Florida. The best summary of this work is Deagan's (1983) *Spanish St. Augustine: The Archaeology of a Colonial Creole Community*. She formulates a cultural pattern for the residents of this colonial outpost. On the basis of archaeological evidence accumulated over the last decade, she suggests that the processes involved in the formation of the Hispanic-American tradition in St. Augustine were common to much of the Spanish New World (1983: 271). Spanish traits were retained in those socially visible areas associated with male activities. This conservatism was coupled with Spanish-Indian acculturation in the less visible, female-dominated areas of daily activity. She goes on to suggest that this pattern of behavior should be expected in any situation where a predominantly male group imposes itself on a group with a normal sex distribution. The data recovered from Puerto Real are used in this study to test this hypothesis. The data are also used to gain a better appreciation of the lifeways of the *vecinos* (Spanish colonists) who lived there. How did they live? What did they eat? What native customs did they adopt, if any? These are all questions that archaeology can help answer.

The material recovered from the 1984–85 excavations at Puerto Real represents only part of the database that will be used to compare with the St. Augustine pattern. Puerto Real appears to have been a grid-pattern town of more than fifty masonry structures (designated during the field investigations as masonry Loci 1–57) situated around a central plaza. The most recent work was conducted at a structure in the northern part of the town, designated Locus 19. Excavations in the plaza area of Puerto Real were carried out in 1979 and 1980, locating two large stone buildings and a cemetery (Willis 1981, Marrinan 1982). Test excavations were performed in 1981 at areas where previous testing had indicated the existence of a range of variability in the status of the inhabitants. These areas included one believed to have been used for beef-and-hide processing (Reitz 1982) and a domestic-occupation site judged to represent a wealthy Spanish household (McEwan 1983). The latter area is of particular interest in that it can be used for comparative purposes with the material recovered by the author of this book from a similar residence.

Testing the Deagan hypothesis requires a series of test implications. One is: "What would we expect to find if the hypothesis is correct?" In archaeology, the material assemblage is a limiting factor. It forces the investigator to rephrase the question to "What would we expect to find *preserved* if the hypothesis is true?" Because the evidence is often fragmentary and incomplete, the archaeologist must extract all possible information from the archaeological record. This means examining every aspect of the data recovered. Without discussing the specifics of the test implications for the hypothesis, it is possible to describe various aspects of the archaeological record and point out their value to the interpretation of the site.

Artifacts are the building blocks of induction for the archaeologist. At Puerto Real, the artifact assemblage has been divided into twenty functionally specific categories for comparative purposes (table 6.1). These categories will be further discussed in chapter 6 along with the artifacts included within each category. Ceramics are a key category because previously they have provided both a chronological framework and indication of the owners' statuses. Similarly, nonceramic artifacts, such as glass, tools, and weaponry, can be used to suggest their owners' relative status, occupations, and ethnic affiliations. In addition, certain artifacts (i.e., food preparation items and types of tablewares) give clues as to the types of diet enjoyed by the site's occupants. However, this particular information can be obtained in other ways.

The faunal assemblage can allow the researcher to make a good assessment of the meat portion of the Spanish colonist's diet. Of particular interest is the proportion of the diet that is made up of indigenous species (fish, turtles, and fowl) as opposed to introduced domesticated species (swine, cattle, and chickens). Is differential use of various species a sign of status differences, preferences based on ethnicity, or simply an adaptation through time to a new environment? Another question that can be addressed using the faunal assemblage is the effect the New World environment had on the domestic species that were introduced. Historical records indicate that the cattle thrived in an environment of extensive, ungrazed pastures, few parasites, and no natural predators (besides humans). The effects of this bovine utopia should show up in the faunal assemblage as skeletal evidence denoting larger and healthier individuals.

Another aspect of Spanish colonial adaptation is in the realm of architecture and urban design. Were the houses Spanish or aboriginal in design? What materials were used to build the structures and what factors influenced their selection? The grid pattern was the hallmark of Spanish colonial town planning, but had not been officially decreed until 1573 (Crouch et al. 1982:xviii). The excavation of Puerto Real provided an opportunity to check whether this decree was issued to correct haphazard town planning or was merely a formalization of a de facto urban design.

Using the data collected form the 1984–85 project and previous work done at Puerto Real, it will be possible in this volume to formulate a tentative "Puerto Real pattern" of Spanish colonial adaptation. The presence of Early Period (pre-1550) and Late Period (post-1550) occupation loci at the site facilitates diachronic analysis of the material to detect the rate of "crystallization" of the pattern. Having delineated a pattern of adaptation at Puerto Real, this will then be compared to that derived from data obtained from St. Augustine. The comparison of these two patterns will make it possible to detect the effects that different economic and environmental factors have on colonial culture formation. Ultimately, it should be possible to make some definitive statements concerning Spanish colonial adaptations to the New World.

2

From Seville to Puerto Real and Points in Between

The documentary record for the colonization of the Caribbean in general during the sixteenth century is, on the whole, fairly extensive. Unfortunately, this does not apply to Puerto Real in particular. It was an economic backwater almost from the beginning and has not merited a great deal of historical research. Many of the pertinent documents that have been discovered were located by Dr. Eugene Lyon in the *Archivo General de las Indias,* in Seville, Spain (Lyon 1981).

Recounting the events that took place at Puerto Real will tell what happened at the site but not why these events took place. To understand the history of Puerto Real—why it was founded, why it was neglected by the Crown, and then forcibly evacuated less than a century later—it is necessary to look beyond the city limits. That is, to put events in their proper perspective, it is essential to know what was happening throughout the Hispanic world during the sixteenth century.

Spain

On the eve of Columbus's departure for the New World, Spain had completed the final stage of its reconquest of the Iberian peninsula: victory over the kingdom of Granada. To some historians, the imperial designs of Spain in America were merely a logical extension of the *Reconquista,* which had begun back in A.D. 718 near the caves of Covadonga in the Cantabrian mountains of northwestern Spain (McAlister 1984:3). This *Reconquista* was not a well-organized, conscious crusade to oust the Moors, but rather a centuries-long series of gains and losses by small Christian kingdoms fighting against each other as well as against the Moslem occupants of Spain. Thus, Spain was not and would not be a unified nation until well into the sixteenth century.

The first steps toward integration were taken in 1469, when Isabella of Castile married Ferdinand, heir to the crown of Aragon. Although neither monarch ever tried to join the two kingdoms officially into a single administrative unit, their joint reign informally achieved this end. An important factor in the creation of a national, unified spirit was the royal effort to cleanse Spain of its perceived ethnic and religious "impurities." In the wake of the fall of Granada in 1492, all Jews residing in the country were ordered to convert to Catholicism or leave. A decade later, the Moors still residing in the peninsula had to make the same decision. Conversion, though, did not guarantee acceptance into society. *Conversos,* as the new Christians were called, were discriminated against at every turn. The establishment of the Spanish Inquisition attempted to abolish all social deviation by enforcing a policy of religious intolerance and *limpieza de sangre* (purity of blood). That instability still existed was evidenced by the turmoil for succession after Isabella's death in 1504. After much difficulty and intrigue, Ferdinand was able to rule both Castile and Aragon until his grandson Charles (the son of Joanna the Mad and Phillip of Austria) came of age.

Charles I was Spanish neither by birth nor inclination. His formative years were spent in Burgundy, in southern France. In 1517, when he arrived in Spain to claim his inheritance, he was young, inexperienced, unaccustomed to the ways of the country, and did not speak the language (Lynch 1984:38). He was already the king of the Low Countries (Luxembourg, Brabant, Flanders, Holland, Zeeland, Hainault, and Artois), when, upon the death of his grandfather Maximilian in 1519, he inherited the Hapsburg's estates of Austria, Tyrol, and parts of southern Germany. His last inheritance allowed him to assume the title of Emperor Charles V.

The Holy Roman Empire, as the realms of Charles V were called, was extensive and included Spain, the Low Countries, Germany, Austria, parts of Italy, and outposts in North Africa. Charles was an ambitious monarch and dreamed of uniting all of Europe under his reign. This had unfortunate consequences not only for Spain but also for its colonies in the New World. First, because his domains were so vast, Charles had little time to devote exclusively to Spain. He spent only sixteen years of his forty-year reign actually residing there (Elliott 1963:154). Secondly, the size of his empire and ambitions dictated that he was almost constantly at war, sometimes on as many as three different fronts. These wars were costly and drained Spain's resources to the point of bankruptcy (this did, in fact, happen three times during his son's reign). Spain's fledgling New World colonies were seemingly viewed as little more than a source of wealth that could be spent on European wars.

Because the government and development of the New World colonies were low on the emperor's list of priorities, their administration was turned over to one of his counselors, Juan Rodriguez de Fonseca, then archdeacon of Seville. The commercial aspects of the colonies were handled by the *Casa de Contratacion*, but Fonseca remained in overall command until his death in 1524. The Council of the Indies was then created to administer the colonies (Elliott 1963:165).

Meanwhile, Charles had needed to cope with a civil war in Castile when the *comuneros* (middle classes) revolted in 1520. This revolution was ostensibly to protect the old way of life in Castile. Most Spaniards, especially Castilians, regarded Charles as a Burgundian interloper who shipped wealth out of their country and replaced it with foreign ministers. The revolt, however, was disorganized and lacked the support of the powerful nobility, who were more afraid of the *comuneros* than of a foreign monarch. The defeat of the *comuneros* in 1521 secured the Hapsburg dynasty in Spain (Elliott 1963:149).

When Phillip II, son of Charles V, inherited the empire in 1556, he also inherited a war with the Pope and France. The following year, he was forced by the Spanish state bankruptcy of 1557 to make peace and abandon the imperial policy of Charles V (Lynch 1984:179). In contrast with the warrior-king Charles V, Phillip II, the supreme bureaucrat, spent his reign ruling from Spain. This change "fittingly symbolized the transformation of the Spanish empire as it passed out of the age of the conquistador into the age of the civil servant" (Elliott 1963:160). It was from Spain that Phillip directed the ill-fated attempts to hold together the empire and crush the rising forces of Protestantism.

This is not to say that Phillip II's tenure as king of Spain was a disaster. On the contrary, Lynch (1984:184) refers to him as "the hardest working monarch in history." Phillip reorganized the government to rule the empire more efficiently. However, widespread corruption and his insistence on personally authorizing virtually every official decision prevented this system from operating as smoothly as it could have. Nevertheless, it was an improvement. Militarily and diplomatically, some notable achievements were made. The *Moriscos* (Christianized Moors residing in Spain) were quickly put down after an attempted revolt in 1568. At Lepanto, in 1571, the Ottoman Empire was beaten at sea and the Mediterranean was made more secure. Finally, in a series of shrewd maneuvers, Phillip was able to gain the crown of Portugal and thus, in 1580, united the entire Iberian peninsula under one ruler.

Unfortunately, Phillip II's personal ability was not sufficient to make Spain an economic or military success. The defeat of the "invincible" Armada (1588) and loss of the Netherlands tarnished Spain's military image. These disastrous military campaigns and the dismal domestic industrial picture resulted in three bankruptcies during Phillip's reign (1557, 1575, and 1596).

Broken both physically and spiritually, Phillip II died in 1598. His son, Phillip III, inherited a nation that needed a capable ruler to pull it out of its decline, but the youth did not possess his father's drive or acumen. Spain would never regain its key position in world affairs.

Spain never dominated the Western world in commerce as it had militarily and politically. Most Spaniards regarded commerce as they did manual labor, a degrading activity to be avoided if possible (Pike 1972). This ethos explains, in part, why the country did not evolve into an industrial power. The economy, never very strong, changed throughout the sixteenth century. The following discussion will be primarily concerned with Castile's role in the Spanish economy because this bears most directly on New World affairs.

The roots of sixteenth-century Spain's economy are to be found in the wool trade. By 1300, when a superior breed of merino sheep was introduced, Castile became the leading wool producer in the international market. The *Mesta* (stockmen's guild) was formed in 1273 by Alfonso X. Although it later became a powerful political entity, the chief duty of the *Mesta* was to organize and maintain the *cañadas* (sheep trails) that ran between the summer and winter pastures (Vicens Vives 1969:253). The Crown's pastoral bias worked to the detriment of Spain's agricultural efforts, but the tax base represented by the *Mesta* was too tempting to resist.

Wool was the principal but not the only export of Spain. Iron was mined and forged in the north, and cloth was made from Castilian wool in the central region. Between 1492 and 1560, Spain was exporting quicksilver, wine, cloth, and luxury items (Vicens Vives 1969:326). The quicksilver (used in the amalgamation of silver ore), wine, and cloth were bound primarily for the American colonies. Spain exported raw materials and metals, relying on imports for most of its manufactured goods, its own industry being very limited in scope. Hence, as is exemplified by Seville, Spanish industry was geared more toward quality production of luxury goods than of utilitarian goods (Pike 1972:131). This would have a significant effect on Spain's mercantilistic relationship with its colonies.

The impact of the New World on the Spanish economy was considerable. The colonies represented wealth in a number of different forms. First, as a source of precious metals, they were unsurpassed. European mining virtually ceased after the opening of the Mexican and Peruvian mines, being unable to compete in either cost or quantity with New World silver and, to a lesser extent, gold. An unfortunate repercussion of this huge influx of wealth was a staggering inflation rate known as the "price revolution" in Spain (Vicens Vives 1969:379).

The colonies supplied a number of other items besides bullion. Hides from the Indies revived the leather-working industry in Spain, which had been initiated by the Moors. Ornamental leather goods, jackets, and the famous gloves of Ocaña and Ciudad Real were made from West Indian hides and sold throughout Europe (Lynch 1984:125). Other imports included cochineal, indigo, dyewoods, sugar, pearls, and plants such as *Cassia fistula* (used as a purgative). Many of the West Indian imports paused only briefly in Seville before becoming part of Spain's export trade.

The preceding statements concerning the thriving wool trade and glut of precious metals and tropical products beg the following question: "Why was Spain perpetually on the verge of bankruptcy?" The answer is simply that its expenses outstripped its income. The next question, then, is: "Where did the money go?"

Much of the wealth was used to supply Spain with goods and services not produced domestically. The country's pro-*Mesta* policies meant that it was constantly importing food to supplement its meager agricultural production. Also, as previously mentioned, the industrial capabilities were not much better than the agricultural base, forcing Spain to rely on other nations' industries for finished products. Even in its trade with the Americas, the country lost potential revenue to foreigners. As Vicens Vives (1967:98) states:

> Genoese bankers monopolized the profits from the exploitation of American mines; Genoese outfitters controlled the provisioning of the fleets. Meanwhile, Italian, Flemish, and French merchants seized control of the colonial trade by means of the fairs at Medina del Campo and the embarkations from Seville and Cadiz.

The trade deficit and foreign domination of trade robbed Spain of much of its potential wealth, but they were not the primary drain on the economy.

Most of Spain's revenue went either to the pursuit of imperial conquests or defense from foreign and internal enemies. Since the *Reconquista,* Spain had been almost continuously at war with at least one adversary, frequently with multiple foes. Charles V initiated many of these costly wars. Elliott (1963:191) describes the long-term effects of this monarch's aggressive policies on the treasury:

> Charles's appeals to the generosity of his subjects and his constant recourse to loans from bankers managed to stave off disaster, but the price paid was a renunciation of any attempt to organize Imperial finances on a rational basis and to plan a coherent economic program for the various territories of the Empire.

The situation did not improve under the reign of Phillip II; if anything, it worsened.

Along with costly foreign campaigns came a concomitant rise in the costs of defensive measures that had to be taken against Spain's growing list of adversaries. In Europe, this meant that a standing army had to be continuously maintained. As the sixteenth century progressed, Spain came to have another realm to protect, the Caribbean.

Little royal funding went to the exploration and settlement of the New World. These activities were accomplished primarily at the personal expense of the conquistadors in return for shares of the colonial revenue. Thus, initially the Crown realized a large return on a very small investment. Lynch (1984:155) aptly summarized the significance of this income: "Trade between Spain and the Indies in the 16th and first half of the 17th century, both in value and the volume of goods carried, was the biggest trans-oceanic trade in the world. It became the most important single item in Spain's economy." However, as American silver began to pour into Spain, other nations started to take an interest in the source of this treasure, forcing Spain to protect its resource base.

The depredations of first French and later English and Dutch interlopers in the Caribbean obliged Spain to take costly and only partially successful defensive measures. These measures included the establishment of a convoy system to protect the treasure fleets and the construction of harbor defenses at key ports in the Caribbean (e.g., Santo Domingo, Cartegena, and Havana). The convoy system functioned well in that it generally protected the fleets from attack. The consequences of the convoy system on Caribbean demographics will be discussed later. The harbor defenses were less successful, each of the main ports being sacked at least once in its history. Successful or not, these defenses were expensive and required regular upkeep as well as sufficient manpower to maintain any sort of effectiveness.

The preceding paragraphs have outlined the history and motivations of the Spanish elite, but what of the rest of the society? Who were the people that settled the New World and how did they behave before they arrived there?

Spain, despite the efforts of the Crown and the Inquisition, was a heterogeneous society throughout the sixteenth century. Castilians, Basques, Catalans, and other groups all had distinctive cultural traits that make most generalizations invalid. Because the province of Andalusia, especially the city of Seville, contributed the most to the early colonization effort (Boyd-Bowman 1976), this region will serve as the basis for the description of Spanish life in the sixteenth century. Pike's (1972) work *Aristocrats and Traders: Sevillian Society in the 16th Century* is an excellent reference for this topic.

Sevillian society was polarized into elites and commoners. Very little existed in the way of a true middle class. The elite was composed of six subcategories: nobles, clergy, lawyers, medical practitioners, notaries, and merchants. Of these, the professionals occupied the most fluctuating and insecure status in the elitist social hierarchy. The clergy's status was secure but had a "ceiling" above which, in theory, they could not aspire. The individuals who had the potential to win and lose the most wealth were the merchants.

Many, if not most, of them were of *converso* origin. Under the doctrine of *limpieza de sangre* in effect at the time, all *conversos* were discriminated against economically and were excluded from public and clerical office (Elliott 1963:218). Naturally, many of them tried to avoid this distinction by commissioning elaborately forged family genealogies and purchasing titles to nobility.

The nobility, on the other hand, by virtue of their pure lineage, had assured social status but were often impoverished. They solved their financial difficulties by either going into business for themselves or marrying into one of the wealthy merchant (i.e., *converso*) families. This symbiotic relationship benefited the nobles by enriching their coffers and the merchants by legitimizing their status. So common were these unions, claims Pike (1972:213), that "by the middle of the 16th century, the majority of the Sevillian nobility consisted of recently enobled families of mixed social and racial origins whose commercial orientation and activities reflected their mercantile background."

On the next social level, the working classes struggled with much less success to better their social position. Including artisans and unskilled laborers, they were generally looked down upon because they performed what was considered manual labor. *Conversos* dominated the upper-level crafts (e.g., pharmacists, silversmiths, clothing makers). These craftsmen were organized by the government into tightly regulated guilds, of which there were about sixty. The creation of these guilds had the effect of stifling free enterprise while forming an easily taxable entity for the Crown (Defourneaux 1979:93–94). Outside the guilds were the unskilled laborers, who were only slightly higher in status than the unassimilated classes.

At the bottom of the hierarchical ladder were the unassimilated classes (*Moriscos*, slaves, and the underworld). The free *Moriscos* (Moors who had converted to Christianity) usually earned their living as stevedores, bearers, and occasionally as farm laborers. The majority of this group were only nominally Christians, retaining their traditional dress and customs. These differences prevented them from becoming fully integrated into Sevillian society. Blacks, on the other hand, adopted Catholicism and Spanish ways and so fared better.

The underworld held a unique place in the society of Seville. Known as *picaros*, these thieves and rogues had informal unions of their own. They were attracted to the city by the riches of the Indies trade (Defourneaux 1979:88). It is tempting to speculate that not a few of these *picaros* found their way to the source of the New World treasure by signing on ships bound in that direction.

Judging by the number of different classes of people and the disparity in wealth, any attempt to describe the range of housing, dress, and food habits would seem to be beyond the scope of this work. Yet, some broad generalizations can be made in regard to these issues.

Spain in the sixteenth century had become a powerful world force not only economically and militarily, but in fashion as well. According to Braudel (1985:320), the European upper classes adopted an austere costume inspired by Phillip II's Spain. The male ensemble consisted of dark material fashioned into close-fitting doublets, padded hose, short capes, and high collars edged with a small ruff. This began to change in the seventeenth century as the French penchant for brighter colors became more popular. Even then, official decorum insisted on the traditional dark Spanish outfit being worn at court. Peasants, on the other hand, do not appear to have been slaves to fashion. Their rough shirts and hose changed little through time.

The eating habits of the Spaniards were, not surprisingly, tied directly to level of affluence, varying from the multicourse fetes of the nobility to the meatless gruels of the abject poor. Yet, despite the differences in content, the main meal for both the affluent and the poor was taken at noon, and no hot food was served in the evening (Defourneaux 1979:152).

Prior to 1550, meat of all kinds was relatively abundant throughout Europe. This was due to the catastrophic population losses of the plagues of the previous centuries (Braudel 1981:190–94). As populations recovered, meat became a less regular part of the peasant diet. Defourneaux (1979:103) characterized the peasant's stable diet as consisting of rye bread, cheese, onions, and in Andalusia, olives. Milk and butter were scarce. Meat, when available, was served in *empanadillas*, small turnovers filled with an unspecified type of meat.

For the upper classes, meat occupied an essential place in the diet. It was commonly prepared in the form of stew or marinated in spices (e.g., pimiento, garlic, or saffron). Favorite dishes included *olla podrida* (meat stew) and *blancmange* (chicken in cream sauce), as well as roast of lamb and beef (Defourneaux 1979:152). Fish was an important feature in the Catholic diet because of the many meatless days. Many freshwater as well as marine species were caught and shipped, on mule back, throughout Spain. Despite smoking, drying and salting the catch, spoilage was a common problem (Braudel 1981:219).

Cumbaa (1975:45) points out that the difference between the food of the peasant and the well-to-do was mainly one of degree. That is, the peasants usually ate a vegetable-laden stew *(puchero)*, and the elite dined on the heartier, spice laden *olla podrida*. All classes were partial to chocolate, which became widely available after the discovery of the Americas.

Housing, like food habits, also differed more in degree than in kind. The exteriors of nearly all houses were plain; any decorative attention was on the interior. In Andalusia, where Arab influence persisted, the upper-class residence was built of brick or stone around a central patio. The houses of the peasants were simpler, being constructed of mud and often consisting of only a single room. Furniture was sparse in sixteenth-century Spain, even among the upper classes; thus, the house interiors must have been by to-day's standards generally stark in appearance. The wealthy had a few costly items of furniture and many carpets and tapestries. In a country with little in the way of wood, this is not unusual. The peasant home, as described by Defourneaux, (1979:103) was even simpler:

> The furniture comprised a roughly made table and some wooden benches. The beds often consisted only of a simple plank or one simply slept on the floor. In a corner of the main room was the hearth, where occasionally a brushwood fire was lit—nearly every-where wood was rare and expensive.

The hearth, a brazier, was the principal source of warmth in all Spanish homes. Wood, charcoal, and even olive pits were burned (Defourneaux 1979:149). Along with oil lamps and candles, the hearths also provided some light. In sixteenth-century Spain, win-dows were not covered with glass, but they were shuttered and some had coverings of paper or oiled, thin parchment. Floors were of bare earth, tile, and/or were covered with mats or Oriental car-pets, depending on the wealth of the inhabitants.

The preceding historical and ethnographic portrait of Spain provides a backdrop for an examination of colonial life in the Ca-ribbean. Only by knowing the history and habits of the colonizing peoples can their responses to what they encountered be properly understood.

The West Indies

The historic period in the Caribbean began with the arrival of Christopher Columbus. The intent of his first voyage was the dis-covery of a western route to the spice islands of the East Indies. In this, he failed completely, though he stubbornly refused to admit his error for the rest of his life (Morison 1942:385).

The exact route of Columbus's first voyage is a matter of much speculation and heated debate. The traditional site of the first land-fall has been Watling's Island, renamed San Salvador to commemorate the event (Morison 1942:222–36). However, a recent investigation, which used computers to take into account the effects of ocean currents and winds, proposes Samana Cay as the most likely candidate for the landing (Judge and Stanfield 1986). Other designations for the site have been made, but it is sufficient here simply to know that Columbus proceeded through the Bahamas to Cuba (which he mistook for mainland China) and turned east and traveled along the north coast of Hispaniola.

It was along the north coast of Haiti where an event took place that pertains directly to the research for this book. On Christmas Eve, 1492, the *Santa Maria* ran aground on a barrier reef just east of the present city of Cap Haitien. The crew was able to reach shore safely, but the ship was a total loss. After negotiations with the native cacique Guacanagari, Columbus decided to leave thirty-nine men to found a small settlement while he went back to Spain. The settlement was named La Navidad in honor of the season. According to Morison (1942:306):

> Navidad fort was built largely of Santa Maria's planks, timbers and fastenings, and provided with a "great cellar" for storage of wine, biscuit, and other stores salvaged from the flagship. Seeds for sowing crops and a supply of trading truck to barter for gold were also left.

Columbus returned a year later to find that the settlement had been torched and all the settlers were dead or missing. The reasons for the massacre are believed to be the Spaniards' greed and mistreatment of the local inhabitants.

Ongoing research by the University of Florida (Deagan 1986) has located what appears to be the village of Guacanagari, within which the site of La Navidad was located. This site, if it is indeed the location of La Navidad, is within 1.5 km of the site of Puerto Real. Whether the fact that the Spanish returned to the same area ten years after the failure of their first colonial attempt is a coincidence or a deliberate act will have to await the discovery of more documentation before it can be answered.

Columbus's first voyage set in motion forces that affected and continue to affect the world to this day. This interaction of the New World with the Old has been labeled the "Columbian Exchange."

Alfred Crosby, who coined the term in a book of the same name (1972:219), renders a harsh verdict concerning the consequences of this exchange:

> The Columbian exchange has included Man, and he has changed the Old and New Worlds sometimes inadvertently, sometimes intentionally, often brutally. It is possible that he and the plants and animals he brings with him have caused the extinction of more species of life forms in the last four hundred years than the usual processes of evolution might kill off in a million. . . . We, all of the life on this planet, are the less for Columbus, and the impoverishment will increase.

Columbus made three other voyages to the Caribbean. The 1493 voyage was specifically to settle the island of Hispaniola, and was successful after a fashion. The third and fourth voyages, in 1498 and 1502, respectively, were exploratory ventures aimed at finding the riches of what the explorer thought was Asia. If he was adept at exploration, he was equally inept at the administration of what he had discovered. This task would be left to the more capable and ruthless Spaniards who were to follow. Relating some of their activities illustrates the historical setting in which Puerto Real developed.

Even while Columbus conducted his third and fourth reconnaissance efforts, other Spaniards were making their own voyages of discovery in the Caribbean. According to Sauer (1966:108), at least four voyages took place in 1499: those of Alonzo de Hojeda, Peralonso Niño, Vicente Yanez Pinzón, and Diego de Lepe. It was Peralonso Niño who discovered the pearl coast of Venezuela that Columbus just missed on his third voyage. After the turn of the century, the entire Caribbean was explored and its major islands and adjoining mainland settled. *Tierra Firme* (or the Spanish Main), as the southern mainland portion of the Caribbean was called, was an early site of intensive exploitation, but not much settlement.

Early colonization efforts focused on the Caribbean islands. In 1508 Sebastian de Ocampo circumnavigated Cuba, proving it to be an island. Three years later, Diego Velazquez, then lieutenant governor of Hispaniola, undertook the task of settling Cuba. The following year, in 1512, Ponce de Leon savagely subdued Puerto Rico and used it as a base for his ill-fated expedition to Florida. During this period of early exploration, Hispaniola served as a point of departure. As the emphasis of colonization shifted to the west, Cuba became the base for the conquistadores. As early as 1519, Hispaniola had already begun to assume a lesser role in the affairs of the Caribbean.

The Caribbean, at the time of the earliest Spanish involvement, was wholly subservient to Spain. The keyword that describes the relationship between that country and the New World is *exploitation*. According to McAlister (1984:81), the Crown and its subjects had similar but conflicting interests:

> The Crown wished to convert and patronize the indigenous population, establish exclusive sovereignty in its American possessions and, at the same time gain a profit from the enterprise. Conquerers and settlers wanted to exploit the natives, acquire senorios, and become wealthy.

The result was that the Indies were developed only to the point of being profitable to the investor.

Most sought after were the precious metals, particularly gold. Columbus was one of the first to voice its importance: "Gold is the most precious of all commodities . . . and he who possesses it has all he needs in the world, as also the means of rescuing souls from purgatory, and restoring them to the enjoyment of paradise" (quoted in McAlister 1984:80–81). However, gold from the islands was never very substantial and was quickly superseded by the major deposits in the mainland, which prompted a gold rush there. For the second time (the decline of the native population being the first), the islands were depopulated; the Caribbean economy reorganized around less-profitable commodities.

For a livelihood, the Spaniards remaining on the islands turned to agriculture and animal husbandry. Crops such as manioc were grown on large estates. The cassava bread made from manioc flour was used as a ship's store, as a staple food for native and African laborers, and to supply early exploratory expeditions. Other subsistance crops such as maize, tropical fruits, yams, beans, and squash were also raised (Parry and Sherlock 1971:15).

Some plants were grown strictly for profit. Of these cash crops, sugar occupied the primary position. Sugarcane had been among the plants brought by Columbus on his second voyage (Sauer 1966:209), but was not grown commercially for another twenty years. Once started, though, production spread rapidly so that by 1523 there were twenty-four mills, or *ingenios,* in operation on Hispaniola (Parry and Sherlock 1971:17). Sugar never became the major export in the Spanish West Indies that it would later become for the French and British colonies. The difficulty in obtaining sufficient numbers of slaves and the inability to compete with gold and silver for the limited cargo space on the fleets curtailed production.

Sugar was the most profitable agricultural product, but it was not the only one exported to Spain. The islands produced some cotton, and Sauer (1966:208) mentions the possible existence of an early cotton gin. *Cassia fistula,* a tree whose bark is similar to cinnamon, was promoted but never became very important as an export. Other plants were cultivated for their medicinal, spice, and dye qualities, but formed a small part of the Atlantic trade. Tobacco, native to the West Indies, was grown by small planters, and its cultivation and exportation were not significant until the last quarter of the sixteenth century (Parry and Sherlock 1971:15). More in line with the temperament of the Spanish colonists was the growth of a livestock industry.

As mentioned previously, the economy of Spain was basically a pastoral one. When transferred to the New World, cattle supplanted sheep as the most numerous Iberian domestic animal in the colonies. Cattle proliferation was so phenomenal that, within decades after their introduction, the hunting of wild cattle became a full-time profession.

The settlers derived many products from their extensive herds, leather being the most important. As early as 1512, hides were being exported to Spain, and production continued to increase throughout the century (Macleod 1984:361). Beef was smoked and jerked for shipment; and, unlike his European contemporaries, no colonist ever wanted for meat. Another by-product of the island cattle industry was beef tallow. Both edible and inedible types were produced. The former was derived from crushed and boiled bones and trimmed fats; the latter from cartilage and sinews. Inedible tallow was the basic ingredient in the manufacture of soap and candles (Reitz 1986:325). As sugar and gold production declined, hides became the economic mainstay of the islands and figured prominently in the later illegal trade.

How was the settlement of Hispaniola accomplished so quickly? When the Spanish came to the New World, they did not find an unpopulated, fertile land waiting to be developed by industrious Europeans, but a land already fully populated. And, when the Spaniards did start to modify and exploit their discoveries, they performed very little of the actual physical labor themselves. This was done by the native inhabitants of the so-called virgin lands. These people had been in the Caribbean centuries before Spain was a nation.

The prehistory of the Circum-Caribbean region is an area of dynamic research. Ideas concerning the population's size, origin, movement, and characteristics continue to change with each new addition to the archaeological database. The generally held hypothesis has been that the islands were originally inhabited by a primitive, preceramic people of uncertain origin, sometimes referred to (erroneously) as the Ciboney. They were displaced and/or absorbed by the Arawaks, who migrated northward from the northern coast of South America, probably from eastern Venezuela (Sauer 1966:5). The peaceful and friendly Arawaks, in turn were being overrun by the warlike and cannibalistic Carib, who had made it as far up the island chain as Puerto Rico when Columbus arrived (Parry and Sherlock 1971:3). Different historians vary on the details, but most of them would agree that this scenario generally fits the meager evidence.

One of the former proponents of this scheme, Irving Rouse, has recently taken a different stance on the peopling of the Caribbean. According to him, instead of successive waves of invading cultures, "linguistic and archaeological research . . . indicate that the Island Carib and Taino (Arawak) Indians developed *in situ* as the result of a single population movement from South America around the time of Christ" (1986:153). He further proposes (1986:155) that the point of entry into the Caribbean was not eastern Venezuela, but more likely the Guianas:

> As the Tainos entered the West Indies, they headed for the major streams, settled along their banks some distance from their mouths,

and exploited the resources in the surrounding forests, paying relatively little attention to seafood. The only places in South America where they could have acquired these preferences are in the Orinoco Valley and on the Guiana coastal plain.

This revised hypothesis, as Rouse himself points out, needs further testing before acceptance.

However the aboriginals came to be there, their general social organization and infrastructure base is fairly well understood. Helms (1984:37) groups the Circum-Caribbean area into two major spheres of political interaction: the Spanish Main (northern Colombia, Panama, Costa Rica, and northern Venezuela) and the Greater Antilles (Hispaniola, Puerto Rico, Jamaica, and Cuba), with the less-developed people of the Lesser Antilles, northeastern Venezuela, and Guiana linking them. The denser populations were organized into ranked societies, with commoners and elites being the major social division. Many of the societies had attained chiefdom status by the time of Columbus's arrival. On Hispaniola this was certainly the case.

Andres Morales and Peter Martyr, early sixteenth-century geographers, divided Hispaniola into five provinces based on native territorial boundaries (Sauer 1966). Other historians (cf. Casas) used different schemes to subdivide the island. In any case, the native way of life was the same. Swidden agriculture provided the villages with most of their food. Plants such as manioc, maize, and yams were grown in cleared plots. Protein was consumed primarily in the form of marine species; terrestrial animals were generally small and scattered.

The Spanish were at first welcomed by the natives of Hispaniola. Columbus (in Sauer 1966:32) wrote that he had developed a

> great friendship with the King of the Land [Guacanagari] who took pride in calling me brother and considered me to be such: and even though they should change their mind, neither he nor his people know what arms are . . . and are the most timorous people of the world. So that the men left there (La Navidad) are sufficient to destroy all that country, without danger to their persons if they know how to rule.

Columbus was exaggerating somewhat, as the fate of the Spaniards at La Navidad was to show. Members of the short-lived first settlement of Columbus warned the natives that the colonists were not there simply to trade peacefully. This knowledge, unfortunately, did not allow the natives to alter the fate that was in store for them.

On his second voyage, Columbus founded a settlement only slightly more successful than his first. Ill-conceived in terms of harborage and resources, Isabella survived only so long as no better place could be found. When Santo Domingo was established on the southern coast by Bartholomew Columbus in 1496, Isabela was all but abandoned (Morison 1942:430). The Indians were subjugated and forced to pay an onerous tribute to the conquistadores. It was in the form of gold wherever possible; otherwise, it was paid in spices, cotton, or food (Sauer 1966:90).

This tribute was not the most valuable contribution of the Indians to the Spaniards. Labor was what was needed and was soon forcibly acquired through the agencies of *encomienda* and *repartimiento*. These two systems, though they achieved the same ends, were subtly different (McAlister 1985:personal communication). A *repartimiento* was a division of spoils. Columbus used this technique with the natives of Hispaniola. No restrictions were imposed on the recipient of the *repartimiento,* and this practice was never officially condoned. Its existence was tolerated partly because of the dire need for labor and partly, perhaps, because of the ambiguous humanity of the Indians in the eyes of the Spaniards. An *encomienda,* on the other hand, was the placing of a populated place under a commander, or *encomendero,* who had the right to extract taxes or labor. Labor was not to be forced but rather "induced" from the Indians. The *encomendero* had the added obligation of Christianizing and civilizing his charges. In actual practice, however, these obligations were rarely fulfilled (Lockhart 1969:411–429).

These systems of labor had catastrophic effects on the Indians. The immediate areas of Spanish conquest suffered a precipitous drop in native population. This decimation can be partly explained by the ruthless extremes of the Spaniards during the "pacification" of the island. Other factors were the overwork, abuse, and suicide created by the conditions of *encomienda.* However, the primary agent for the elimination of Hispaniola's natives can be attributed to European-introduced diseases. So great was the population decline that Spanish slaving expeditions were sent to neighboring islands to supplement the work force on Hispaniola (Sauer 1966:159).

The complete subjugation of Hispaniola occurred during the governorship of Nicolas de Ovando (1502–09). With brutal efficiency, he extended the Spanish sway throughout the entire island. The system of *encomienda* was formalized during his tenure. Another of his accomplishments was the founding of fifteen towns on the island (Sauer 1966:151). This had a twofold purpose: it satisfied the royal instruction to establish new settlements, and it also ensured the complete subjugation of the natives. Puerto Real was one of these new communities.

Puerto Real

Much of the basic information for this section is taken from Eugene Lyon's (1981) documentary research at the *Archivo General de las Indias,* in Seville, Spain.

Around 1503 Rodrigo de Mexia, a lieutenant of Governor Ovando, led a group of settlers to the northern coast of Hispaniola to found a new city. The location chosen for this settlement, christened Puerto Real because of its excellent harbor, was very close to the old site of La Navidad (figure 2.1). This time, instead of massacring the natives, the Spanish were successful in bending them to their will.

Puerto Real was originally envisioned as a mining colony. The Spanish lust for gold prompted a brief flurry of mining activity in the mountainous hinterland of Puerto Real (Sauer 1966:154). Unfortunately for the settlers, no gold was found and existing copper deposits proved disappointing. The area around Puerto Real did, however, serve as a source of labor for the more productive mining districts.

Puerto Real's early years were its best ones. During the first decade of the sixteenth century, it was a thriving community of about a hundred households (Haring 1947:207n). In 1508 the Crown granted the settlement its own coat of arms, consisting of a golden

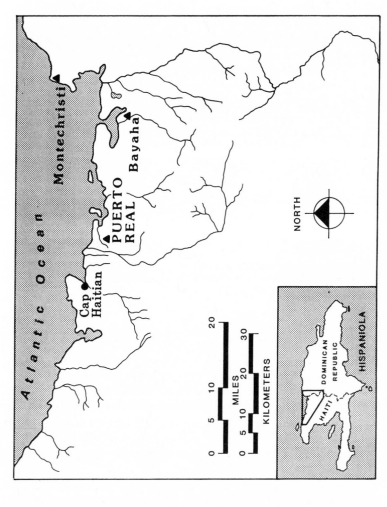

Figure 2.1. Location of Puerto Real (*drafted by Charles Poe*)

Figure 2.2. Coat of Arms of Puerto Real *(drawn by author from a photo at the Council of the Indies Chambers, Santo Domingo)*

ship sailing a wavy sea on a field of blue (figure 2.2). This emblem recalled the arrival of Christopher Columbus in the area in 1492 (Hodges 1980:3). During the early years, the town boomed.

The decline in the native population coupled with the rise in demand for labor prompted Spanish slaving raids on other nearby islands. In the north, the Bahamas were depopulated of their Lucayan inhabitants. Puerto Plata and Puerto Real were the ports servicing these slaving operations (Sauer 1966:159). A total of 40,000 Indians were unloaded at these two ports (Hodges 1980:3). Because these Indians also succumbed to disease and the harsh conditions, African slaves were brought in. The end of the Lucayan trade (ca. 1514) signaled the beginning of a general decline in the towns of the northern coast (Lyon 1981).

Spaniards formed only a comparatively small part of the population. The *repartimiento* of 1514 illustrates the imbalance of the population of Puerto Real. There were only 20 *vecinos* (in this case, probably meaning registered citizens). Of these, three had Castilian wives, and two had native wives. Also mentioned are eighteen other residents who held Indians. The status of these residents is uncertain. Of the 839 Indians listed, 540 were *Indios de Servicio*, which were the original *encomienda* Indians of the island. The other natives were classified as *naborias*, or lifelong serfs. They were not even technically free and may have been the imported Lucayans.

The continuing decline of the north prompted the abandonment of the neighboring town of Llares de Guahaba, whose citizens moved to Puerto Real. The fall of the north corresponded with the situation on the island as a whole and can be traced to the Spanish preoccupation with silver and gold.

After the initial gold frenzy on Hispaniola had died down, it became a base for further exploration. When the real mineral wealth of the New World was discovered on the mainland, the population drain began in earnest (Andrews 1978:54). The mainland gold rush did more than just draw off manpower; it diverted shipping away from the less-profitable island ports.

The convoy system of shipping, established in 1542, was designed to ensure that the precious metals from Mexico and Peru arrived safely in Spain. All ships were required to sail in convoy and visit only the ports on the convoy's route. One need only glance at the routes of the treasure fleets (figure 2.3) to see that Puerto Real is located well away from the *Carrera de las Indias*. Denied access to regular shipping, Puerto Real and the other neglected island ports turned to the *rescate* (illegal trade) for goods.

Meanwhile, on land, the citizens of Puerto Real had needed to contend with other problems. A smallpox epidemic swept the island in 1518–19, nearly wiping out the Arawak population (Lyon 1981). Puerto Real came to depend more upon imported African labor. So great was the demand that by 1520 these slaves had become the dominant element in the work force (Andrews 1978:11–12).

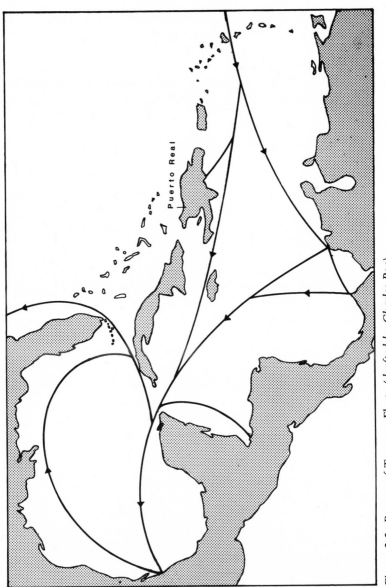

Figure 2.3. Routes of Treasure Fleets *(drafted by Charles Poe)*

The Indians do figure later in the history of Puerto Real. In 1519 under chief Tamayo they revolted around the environs of Puerto Real. They later joined with the general revolt led by the cacique Enrique. As late as 1532, hostilities persisted when a *vecino*, his wife, two children, and fourteen of his Indian slaves were killed. Peace was finally achieved the following year. That same year, sixty colonists arrived in Santo Domingo to repopulate Puerto Real and Monte Christi, located to the east.

By this time, the economy of Puerto Real and the islands in general was based upon the hide trade. Leather was much in demand in Europe, and the Indies possessed an abundance of cattle. The mercantile policies of Spain decreed that all colonial commerce should be conducted exclusively with the mother country. Unfortunately, bulky hides could not compete with silver and gold for the limited cargo space of the fleets.

Such was the paradox that confronted the citizens of Puerto Real. They could obey the law and do without even the barest necessities, or they could trade with smugglers and enjoy European goods unavailable to them by other means. Another consideration was the trading practices of the smugglers, who were not above transacting business at gunpoint. Often the choice would be to trade with the corsairs or risk having the town sacked and burned by them. In 1566 the French corsair Jean Bontemps entered Monte Christi, Puerto Real, and La Yaguana. He seized twelve vessels and set the torch to Puerto Real (Andrews 1978:96). Not surprisingly, most of the hides produced at Puerto Real found their way into the illegal trade system.

The chief perpetrators of the *rescate* changed throughout the sixteenth century. According to Lyon (1981), prior to the mid-sixteenth century most of the foreign interlopers were Portuguese, who dealt mainly in slaves. Frenchmen, present as early as 1535, were heavily involved in smuggling after 1548. John Hawkins, the renowned corsair, and other Englishmen were operating in the islands after 1560. The Dutch did not become important in the *rescate* until the end of the century, but their presence eventually forced the abandonment of the western half of Hispaniola (Andrews 1978:174).

Meanwhile, Puerto Real had been suffering from both natural

and economic disasters. In 1562 an earthquake rocked the northern coast of Hispaniola. This was followed by the French corsair raid in 1566. That same year, Spain ordered a cessation of registry of ships at Puerto Real because of the smuggling activities there. The town sued and had its registry temporarily restored, but this only delayed the inevitable.

Ironically, it was not the loss of revenue that worried the Spanish Crown. The economic importance of the hide trade was negligible. Andrews (1978:195) claims that "hides were the virtual offal of the Indies, left for Lutherans and mulattoes to haggle over by Spaniards occupied with transactions of a higher order—in sugar, dyes and precious metals." Rather, the main concern of the Crown was the *presence* of these foreign interlopers, *not* in the hides they diverted from Spain.

In the ports of northern and western Hispaniola, practically the whole population was involved in smuggling (Andrews 1978:208). Spain could not stop this activity (its own Crown-appointed town officials were heavily involved themselves!); neither could it provide adequate shipping for these outpost settlements. In 1578 the settlement of Bayaha was established midway between Puerto Real and Monte Christi and populated with the citizens of the two towns. An armed force was required to coerce the resettlement. It was thought that stopping the smuggling at a single point would be easier than all along the coast. However, this was not the case. Smuggling continued with the collusion of the town officials. Spain's ultimate response was the depopulation of the western third of the island in 1605. This ended the Spanish chapter of Puerto Real and began the French chapter of what was to become Haiti.

3

Previous Archaeological Work

The site of Puerto Real was discovered in 1974 by Dr. William Hodges. A medical missionary in Haiti for more than twenty-five years, he is an avid archaeologist and historian, whose interests are well known to the villagers around Cape Haitian. Many of the local farmers bring him old "treasures" they had found while hoeing their gardens. Hodges, who had been searching for the site of La Navidad, received an important clue when farmers from the nearby village of Limonade showed him some sixteenth-century artifacts they had found. Of particular interest was a worn copper coin. It was identified as a four-maravedi piece, common in the Greater Antilles during the sixteenth century. This led Hodges to conclude that a Spanish settlement had existed in the area, one that was later than La Navidad, established by Columbus in 1492 (Hodges 1980:3).

An examination of the area where the artifacts were found confirmed Hodges's suspicions that this was not the site of La Navidad. Far more artifacts littered the surface than could be accounted for by a small settlement that had lasted for less than a year. In addition to the surface-collected artifacts, several low mounds were found. Excavation of one of these yielded three stone gargoyles and a large quantity of building rubble. One of these gargoyles has the head of an elephant and the body of a sheep or some other hooved animal. Clearly, a substantial settlement had existed in the area. The artifacts indicated that it had a sixteenth-century Spanish provenience. Based on his knowledge of the history of the area, Hodges concluded that the artifacts must be from the sixteenth century Spanish settlement of Puerto Real. His discovery opened an important chapter in New World Spanish colonial archaeology.

Realizing the potential significance of the site, Hodges and M. Albert Mangones (representing the Haitian government) contacted Dr. Charles Fairbanks at the University of Florida, in Gainesville. Fairbanks, a Distinguished Service Professor in Anthropology and internationally known expert on Spanish colonial archaeology, also recognized the importance of the discovery and worked with Hodges and Mangones to establish a project to conduct fieldwork in Haiti. Fairbanks was successful in his efforts, and in 1979 he sent one of his graduate students, Raymond Willis, to lead a crew into the field.

The orientation of all the archaeological research done at Puerto Real is to better understand how the sixteenth-century Spaniards adapted to the New World. This type of long-distance colonizing effort had very little precedent for their nation. What form would its effort take? Adopt New World modes of living? Transplant the Iberian way of life in toto? Synthesize an eclectic mixture of both? Answering these questions has guided all research at Puerto Real, including the current efforts.

The primary goal of the 1979 season was to identify the site positively. It was decided that the best way to do this within the constraints of available time and money was to concentrate on the supposed center of the site, specifically the large rubble pile where the gargoyle had been found. Before actual excavation began, the area was cleared of the thorny brush growing there, and a contour map was made. A preliminary walkover survey of the area was conducted to delineate the site boundaries, and a permanent concrete benchmark that would serve as a reference point for all subsequent excavation grids was emplaced. The contour map revealed that there were actually two mounds: a rectangular-shaped one running roughly north-south; and a square-shaped rise near the northwestern corner of the rectangular mound.

Willis (1984:57) initiated an excavation to discover the nature of the rectangular mound. He decided to bisect it with a north-south trench and cross it with two east-west trenches. Willis and Paul

Hodges (Dr. William Hodges's son) supervised twenty Haitian workers, who excavated thirty-nine 2 x 2 m units. These excavations revealed the remains of what had been a three-room masonry building.

Most of the stone foundation was missing, having been robbed by later peoples for use in their own structures. The trenches they had dug to mine the stone were clearly apparent as dark stains in the buff-colored clay. A large amount of broken brick and roof tile littered both the interior and exterior of the structure. Along with the building rubble, Willis recovered a substantial amount of sixteenth-century Spanish majolica, glass, coins, iron artifacts, and faunal material.

The delineation of such a large structure (27 x 7 m) and the recovery of so many unequivocally datable sixteenth-century artifacts confirmed that the site was Puerto Real. No other settlement of any size is recorded for that time period in the area. A cursory walkover survey of the surrounding area indicated that the site measured nearly 500 x 500 m. Most importantly, except for the robbing of construction material, the site seemed little disturbed by any post-abandonment activity. Today, Haitians living on the site practice hoe agriculture and only disturb the upper 15 cm of the soil. The success of the first season's excavations encouraged the participants to return to the site the following summer.

During the second season (1980) the University of Florida formally entered the project. This allowed a larger-scale archaeological effort. Ray Willis returned with three other graduate student archaeologists (Jennifer Hamilton, Rochelle Marrinan, and Gary Shapiro) from the University of Florida. The crew of Haitian villagers hired as field hands doubled from twenty to forty.

The 1980 field season focused on the complete excavation of Building A, as the structure discovered the previous year had been named. The results were encouraging (Willis 1984:59). Willis interpreted this building as the central cathedral or possibly some other public structure situated on the town plaza (1984:128). Another structure located under the square-shaped mound next to Building A was designated as Building B. The town cemetery was discovered a few meters west of this structure. In the process of putting in a fence post, one of the Haitian workers unearthed a human cranium.

A 2 x 3 m test excavation, directed by Dr. William Hodges, uncovered the remains of three individuals (Willis 1984:65).

A rich and varied array of artifacts was recovered during the 1980 excavations (Willis 1984:156). A wide variety of Spanish majolica as well as the more common utilitarian wares, such as olive jar or green bacin, were found scattered around the exterior of Building A. Some of the most spectacular artifacts came from the test pits used to determine the placement of the trenches. Two of these reconnaissance soundings yielded nearly intact Spanish rapier swords; and, in another, a reconstructable pitcher made of honey-colored melado ware (Willis 1984:262–3). Other nonceramic items collected from the general excavation units included locks, keys, hawk bells, buckles, horse tack, scissors, an ornate book clasp, Venetian glass, and more than 150 coins. All the coins were the four-maravedi pieces described earlier, a coin of small worth even in colonial times, which may account for their ubiquitous presence at the site. Perhaps, like modern pennies, the sixteenth-century Spaniards did not consider them worth bending over to pick up when dropped.

While Willis was working on Building A, the other team members pursued ancillary projects. The topographic-mapping project, under the supervision of Hamilton, was expanded to cover the rest of the central area. She also delineated the site boundaries by laying in a series of linear test-pit transects across the site (Hamilton 1982). Her findings indicated that the town occupied an area measuring 450 m north–south by 400 m east–west.

Test excavation was not the only means used to sample the site. Shapiro conducted a resistivity survey of the area around Building A and was able to produce resistivity contour maps that allowed for accurate prediction of the location of subsurface features (e.g., building foundations; see Shapiro 1984). According to Shapiro (p. 109): "The most important advantage gained by the use of the technique is the ability to save precious excavation time by the prediction of subsurface feature locations, and the ability to generate testable hypotheses concerning site plan." The resistivity maps also allowed Willis to project the dimensions of the buildings he only partially excavated.

In addition to the survey and excavation, a faunal collection of contemporary Haitian vertebrates was prepared. Marrinan supervised this project in an effort to supplement the comparative collections at the Florida State Museum (Willis 1984:67). Most of the specimens collected were marine species of fish, but some terrestrial species were also recovered. These specimens were to be used later to help identify the faunal material recovered from Puerto Real.

Although much was accomplished during the 1980 field season, it became apparent that the surface had literally and figuratively only been scratched. The University of Florida, Organization of American States (OAS), and the Haitian government all reaffirmed their commitment to the Puerto Real project and to continued investigations.

Another large crew conducted field studies during the 1981 season. This time, however, instead of concentrating on one central excavation, they initiated several smaller projects. Rochelle Marrinan directed work at Building B (Marrinan 1982), and Bonnie McEwan (another University of Florida graduate student) and Jennifer Hamilton excavated outlying areas that the previous year's testing and resistivity survey had indicated might be residential structures (Hamilton 1982, McEwan 1983). The results of this season's efforts were productive and, in some cases, enigmatic.

Building B proved to be a thick-walled 8 x 10 m structure whose function could not be positively ascertained. Willis (1984:145) speculates that it was an auxillary to Building A, probably a tower of some sort. Other possibilities include a blockhouse, secure warehouse, or some other public building (Marrinan 1982:54–57). It is not thought to be a residence for several reasons: its massive architecture, its location on the plaza, and the paucity of domestic artifacts recovered from the site. The other two areas excavated did appear to have been habitations, or at least have residential components associated with them.

Loci 33 and 35 (how these loci came to be designated will be discussed later), excavated under the supervision of Bonnie McEwan, appeared to be the location of a high-status residence (McEwan 1983:103). This conclusion is based on the amounts and types of high-quality majolicas, Venetian glass, and faunal remains recovered. In this case, the domestic refuse rather than the structure was the most telling clue as to site function. Very little of the actual structure was excavated. The area excavated appears to be the backyard fence line against which trash had been regularly deposited (McEwan 1983:103).

The most intriguing finds came from the third area excavated during the 1981 field season. Artifacts that Hamilton recovered from Locus 39 seemed, by reference to documented patterns of status variability in St. Augustine (Deagan 1983), to indicate a low-status household. That is, many of the ceramics were crude locally produced wares and expensive glassware as well as decorative artifacts were largely missing from the artifact assemblage. However, the amount and nature of the animal bone refuse recovered seemed out of place for a domestic context, and the site could have been the locus of commercial activities related to cattle.

Elizabeth Reitz, zooarchaeologist now at the University of Georgia, performed the faunal analysis for this area (Reitz 1986). She determined that more than 70 percent of the animal bone recovered was the remains of butchered cattle that had not fully matured. She also noted that the cattle, even though immature, were very large. In fact, the size range overlapped that of aurochs, an extinct bovid believed to be the forerunner of domestic cattle. Reitz attributed this to the fact that, when cattle were introduced into the area by the colonists, they found no native ruminants that could have been vectors for disease or competitors for food; there also were no predators, except humans. Consequently, the cattle attained large size.

It is known from the documents that Puerto Real was a major hide-producing center (Sauer 1966, Lyon 1981, Hoffman 1980). Reitz (1986:327) proposed, from the amount and type of bone elements recovered, that this area of the site was where refuse from skinning and meat preservation was used to make tallow and other cattle industry by-products. The combination of household artifacts and faunal remains indicated that this area may have been used for both residential and commercial use. Reitz also noted that this slaughter/processing area was downwind from most of the town!

The following year (1982) marked a change in supervision of the Puerto Real project. Dr. Kathleen Deagan, former student of Fairbanks and now at the Anthropology Department of the Florida

Museum of Natural History, assumed direction of the project. Her first decision was to suspend any further excavation pending the completion of the reconnaissance testing and contour-mapping program begun in 1980.

A total of 1,475 .25 x .25 m test pits were excavated at 10 m intervals across the site during the 1982 season. The contents were analyzed and the raw data entered into the mainframe computer at the University of Florida. Maurice Williams, Florida State Museum archaeologist and project supervisor, was able to graphically depict horizontal distributions of various types of artifacts using the SYMAP package (a graphic/analytic program) (Williams 1986). This was an important achievement for several reasons. First, it more clearly delineated the town limits than had previous attempts. Secondly, by plotting distributions of masonry debris, Williams was able to define fifty-seven discrete concentrations thought to represent structures within the town's boundaries. By plotting distributions of high- and low- status artifacts and artifacts that could be precisely dated, it was further possible to obtain an idea of economically distinct sections of the town along with demographic shifts through time. These data were invaluable to all subsequent work done at the site and will be elaborated on in chapter 5.

In 1984 another project was sponsored by the Florida State Museum in cooperation with the Organization of American States, the government of Haiti, and the Institute for Early Contact Period Studies at the University of Florida. Specifically, this work was aimed at studying adaptation through time at Puerto Real. To do this, it was necessary to examine a residence occupied during the early years of the town and compare it with an economically similar residence occupied during the latter part of Puerto Real's existence.

Fortunately, the 1984 project was in an ideal position to accomplish this task. Excavations at Loci 33 and 35 in 1981 had provided the necessary data from an Early Period (pre-1550), high-status occupation. The results of the survey in 1982 made it possible to locate a late (post-1550) high-status occupation. The field season in 1984 was spent locating this structure, and the 1985 season was spent excavating it.

4

Theoretical Orientation

The emphasis placed upon much of the research on early Spanish colonialism has been understanding how the colonists adapted themselves and their society to the social and environmental conditions encountered in the New World. Recent historical synthetic works (e.g., Bethell 1984, Lockhart and Schwartz 1983, and McAlister 1984) demonstrate that historians have long addressed this topic. However, historical archaeologists have only just begun to study Spanish colonialism.

This raises the question: "If historians have long been addressing this topic, why should archaeologists bother?" What can the archaeologist hope to add that a legion of historians have not already discovered? The fact that a long line of historians have studied Spanish colonialism partially answers this question. Paradigms within a discipline are constantly changing, and a new perspective brings fresh insight to an old subject. The entrance of historical archaeology into Spanish colonial studies brings yet another approach, an anthropologically oriented one, to bear on this topic.

Archaeology does more than merely offer a new interdisciplinary perspective, which alone would justify the effort. By examining the material record, the archaeologist can examine cultural processes; verify, supplement, or refute the historical record; and generally gain insight into the everyday lives of past peoples. For Puerto Real, this is particularly true.

Few documents pertaining to the town have been discovered or may ever be discovered. Archaeological data can supplement the scant historic record in such areas as foodways, material possessions, architecture, and urban planning. Documents reveal that smuggling was so rampant that the *vecinos* of Puerto Real were relocated. Yet, how is this illicit behavior manifest in the archaeological record, the record of the everyday lives of the people of Puerto Real?

Archaeology is also instrumental in the study of historically disenfranchised groups (e.g., slaves). Descriptions of the everyday life of the Indians and/or slaves are missing from the documents at Puerto Real, and, indeed, from colonial records in general. A good example of the contributions of archaeology in this regard is the work of Charles Fairbanks (1984) at Kingsley plantation, which illuminated aspects of slave society not present in the documentary record.

Historical archaeology is not merely a handmaiden to history. It is an equal partner, using different and additional data to answer questions concerning past human behavior. The problems of culture contact and adaptation have become central to Spanish colonial archaeology. It is also the central theme of the current research.

Spanish efforts to colonize previously unknown territory had very little precedent in the sixteenth century. True, the Canary Islands had been discovered and settled in the previous century and did provide some lessons for the Spaniards. But the distances involved in a transatlantic effort made the colonization of the Americas, by their very remoteness, an essentially new experience.

Having decided to settle Hispaniola, the Spanish had three basic options in regards to settlement strategy. The first one would be complete retention of their Castilian life-style, rejecting any New World-inspired changes. At the other extreme, the colonists could elect to abandon their "civilized" ways and "go native": that is, adopt the cultural behavior of the indigenous peoples in toto. The third, which is based on previous research in St. Augustine, would be a compromise solution: retaining some traits of the original society while incorporating new traits of the non-Hispanic societies and modifying other traits in response to the new circumstances. The result would be a hybrid society, distinct from its predecessors.

If this is the case, the question then becomes one of distinguishing which old traits were retained and which new traits were adopted and why.

The anthropological term used for the changes that come about as a result of culture contact is *acculturation*. But what is meant exactly by this word? Like the term "culture" itself, it is a loosely defined and often abused anthropological concept. Some anthropologists have seen it as a one-way process: "Acculturation occurs when a society undergoes drastic culture change under the influence of a more dominant culture and society with which it has come into contact" (Hoebel 1972).

Originally the term was employed to refer to changes in the culture patterns of either or both groups (Redfield, Herskovits, and Linton 1936). But this second definition is so broad as to have little utility.

Edward Spicer (1961:529) uses acculturation in the general sense: "The augmentation, replacement, or combination in a variety of ways of the elements of a given cultural system with the elements of another." He does, however, go on to define four general types of acculturation: incorporation, assimilation, fusion, and compartmentalization (1961:529–36):

> 1) incorporation—the transfer of elements from one cultural system and their integration into another system in such a way that they conform to the meaningful and functional relations within the latter without disrupting the fundamental system.
> 2) assimilation—acceptance and replacement of cultural behaviors in terms of the dominant society's cultural system.
> 3) fusion—whatever the specific form of combination, the principles which guide it are neither wholly from one or the other of the two systems in contact.
> 4) compartmentalization—a keeping separate within a realm of elements and patterns taken over from the dominant culture.

It is important to note that Spicer (1961:539) sees all forms of acculturation as being preceded by a process of adaptive integration, where nothing important is replaced: that is, an initial acceptance of some new traits (mostly material culture), on a trial basis, which eventually give way to the processes described above. This will have to be taken into account when interpreting the data recovered from Puerto Real. The problem is distinguishing transitory acquisition from incorporation. This can be done by utilizing a diachronic approach, comparing Early to Late Period proveniences.

The cultural exchanges that come about as the result of a contact situation are rarely perfectly reciprocal. Foster (1960:7) insists that the idea of dominance should be included in the operational definition. It is this concept of dominance that is integral to his model of the "conquest culture." In this scenario of culture contact, one society acts primarily as the donor, and the other as the recipient.

The "conquest culture" is a model that represents the totality of donor influences brought to bear on a recipient society. Foster (1960:10–12) states that this is artificial in that what the recipient culture is exposed to represents only a selection from the totality of the donor's culture. The formation of this "conquest culture" is characterized by a stripping-down process in which elements of the dominant culture are modified or eliminated. Thus, using Foster's model, the culture of the Spanish colonists was modified before they landed in the New World.

What were the influences that went into the formation of the colonial "conquest culture"? Foster (1960:12) describes two types of selective processes that are involved. The first of these are formal processes: cognizant, intentional changes where the government, church, or some other authoritative body directs the introduction of selected attributes. An example of this would be the imposition of the grid town plan on the colonists by the Spanish Crown. The second selective process is informal and includes the habits of the emigrants themselves, such as their food preferences, personal beliefs, and attitudes.

Another source of influence upon the "conquest culture" is that of the "conquered culture." Although the major changes are found in the culture of the recipient group, Foster (1960:7) acknowledges that in contact situations the donor group changes to some degree. More emphatically, he states that "during the American conquest, Spanish ways were *profoundly* modified by the existing cultures" (p. 2). The result of these changes (formal, informal, and acquired) has been described as the Spanish colonial pattern. That pattern, as used in this study, is the one suggested through archaeological investigations in St. Augustine.

Early work there was essentially descriptive in nature and dealt with large monuments such as the Castillo de San Marcos (Harrington, Manucy, and Goggin 1955). During the 1950s, serious attention was being directed toward sites of the Spanish colonial inhabitants. Later, following trends already manifest in the new archaeology, Charles Fairbanks (1975) initiated problem-oriented "backyard archaeology," which focused on the everyday life of the average Spanish colonist. From the early 1970s onward, the guiding research orientation was understanding the processes related to the formation and development of the Hispanic-American cultural tradition in Florida. This, as Deagan details,

> encompassed a number of more specific anthropological issues, such as the role of acculturation in these processes, the extent and nature of Spanish-Indian syncretism, the crystallization of a Spanish-American *criollo* tradition, and the understanding of the nature of social variability within it. (1983:53)

Deagan's own work initially (1974) focused on the cultural consequences of intermarriage between Spanish males and Indian females. (The processes of Indian-Spanish miscegenation, called *mestizaje*, were examined at the eighteenth-century de la Cruz site (SA-16-23) in St. Augustine, Florida. Specifically, "the excavation at the de la Cruz site attempted to establish material correlates for the processes of *mestizaje* and acculturation represented at the site" (1974:147). Applying the acculturation models of Spicer (1961 and 1962) and Foster (1960) to historical and archaeological data gathered in St. Augustine, Deagan confirmed the hypothesis that "acculturation in 18th century St. Augustine was effected largely by Indian women in Spanish or *mestizo* household units, within a predominantly male-oriented (military) cultural milieu." As is so common in any scientific endeavor, the process of testing one hypothesis generated new hypotheses.

Based on the data recovered from the de la Cruz household, Deagan (1974:150–52) proposed several hypotheses to be tested as new data became available. The first stated that the initial stages of *mestizaje* would have a preponderance of native elements in those areas of culture associated with female activities, but that these native elements would be quickly replaced by *criollo* or European elements as the *mestizos* became established in the New World society. Secondly, it was hypothesized that the influences on the *mestizo* households were derived from the New World *criollo* culture rather than that of peninsular Spain. Another hypothesis was that the low status of the *mestizo* household is reflected by its segregation into the marginal areas of the town. Finally, Deagan proposed that the diet of the *mestizo* would show a greater use of local resources than would European households.

Unfortunately, at the time of her investigation (1974), little comparative data were available. Excavation of ordinary households in St. Augustine was just beginning. However, the avenues of inquiry opened in Deagan's dissertation would be addressed by future research.

The St. Augustine pattern delineated by Deagan (1983) is a direct outgrowth of her dissertation research (1974). She suggests that early Hispanic colonial adaptive efforts were characterized by the incorporation of locally available elements into the colonist's low-visibility subsistence and technological activities, while at the same time maintaining Spanish affiliation in such socially visible activities and elements as clothing, tableware, ornamentation, and religious paraphernalia. This dichotomous pattern was continued and refined through time, eventually crystallizing into a distinctive Hispanic-American colonial tradition. These patterns were independently linked through documentary analysis to social variation and affiliation in the community.

Based on archaeological evidence accumulated during more than a decade of fieldwork, Deagan (1983:270) suggests that the processes involved in the formation of the Hispanic-American tradition in St. Augustine were common to much of the Spanish New World. Conservatism in those socially visible areas associated with male activities was coupled with Spanish-Indian acculturation in the less-visible, female-dominated areas. Deagan goes on to hypothesize that this pattern of behavior should be expected in any situation where a predominantly male group imposes itself on a group with a normal sex distribution.

Puerto Real is an ideal site to test this hypothesis because a predominantly male group (the Spaniards) imposed itself on a group with a normal sex distribution (the Tainos). The differences in geographic location, relative prosperity, and settlement type (exploitation versus military garrison) between Puerto Real and St. Augustine eliminate these as biasing factors and help to support the contention that this hypothesis represents a truly pan-Hispanic colonial pattern rather than a Spanish, mainland, garrison pattern.

Certain archaeologically testable implications follow from the hypothesized Spanish colonial pattern. Before these test implications are delineated, it is appropriate to discuss the problems of interpreting past lifeways from the archaeological assemblage. Unlike cultural anthropology, much of which interprets from observed behavior, archaeology must work with *preserved* behavior. If cultural anthropology is analogous to working a jigsaw puzzle without the benefit of the picture on the box, then archaeology includes the extra handicap of missing many of the pieces. Nevertheless, many aspects of human behavior are reflected, in some way, in the archaeological assemblage.

Determining how specified properties of past cultural systems can be accurately identified and measured is the domain of middle-range research (Binford 1981:25). Without going into too much detail, this type of research simply involves the determination of how various types of human behavior are represented in the archaeological record. This is what the test implications attempt to do in relation to the patterns of human behavior outlined in the hypothesis. These tests simply state: "If the hypothesis is true, this is what we should expect to find." Should the tests support the hypothesis, this does not exclude the possibility that other interpretations exist for the data. However, it does allow us to continue to use the hypothesis to guide future research. With this in mind, test implications relevant to the hypothesis can be presented.

1. Food preparation activities, as represented in the archaeological assemblage, should show a significant admixture of European and locally manufactured wares. This is as opposed to a total retention of European utilitarian wares. Supply lines between Puerto Real and Spain were tenuous at best. This situation forced the colonists to seek other means of satisfying the need for cooking and storage containers. Using the pottery of the local inhabitants

would have provided an inexpensive answer. Also, the intermarriage of Spanish men with local women offered an avenue for the introduction of these wares because women were most involved with food preparation activities. Non-European utilitarian ceramics, used for cooking and storage of food, as well as manioc griddles and other local elements not typical of the Iberian kitchen assemblage, should demonstrate this dependence.

In the initial stage of colonization, it would be expected that the locally available Taino Indian wares would have been used by the earliest settlers to supplement their utilitarian wares. It would furthermore be anticipated that the nature of the locally manufactured items would have shifted from Indian to African-influenced types through time. As discussed earlier, the Indians of the *encomienda* assigned to Puerto Real declined rapidly as the result of disease and overwork. They were replaced by imported African slaves, who, by 1520, had become the dominant element in the work force. The archaeological record should reflect this shift in ethnic composition by a change in the nature of the utilitarian ceramics as the African potters replaced the Indian potters.

2. Status-related artifacts should be almost exclusively European in trade or manufacture. Spanish colonial status was linked to the closeness of association with peninsular Spain (cf. McAlister 1963, Morner 1967, 1983). It would be expected that the attempts by New World settlers to maintain an Iberian life-style (with its accompanying prestige) would be reflected in the use of articles from the Spanish Empire in socially visible areas of daily life.

Socially visible activities are reflected in many aspects of the material assemblage. A Spaniard's table would be highly visible to neighbors and guests. Following the hypothesis, we would expect the tablewares to be composed primarily of majolica, rather than locally made wares. The higher-status colonist might include such scarce items as porcelain and glassware because he would be able to afford such luxuries.

Similarly, clothing and ornamentation would be Iberian in style, if not manufacture. Most clothing items leave no trace in the archaeological record. However, such Spanish clothing accessories as aglets (lacing tips), buckles, and buttons *would* survive and serve as evidence for the retention of Spanish costume because local clothing (such as existed) did not utilize these items. Ornaments, such as jewelry, would be expected to show a preference for European styling (e.g., clothing adornments, pendants, and rings), though the material from which they were manufactured might have originated in the New World. This is as opposed to the adoption of native design elements and ornaments encountered by the early colonists.

A final category of material culture that would indicate nonacculturation in the socially visible sphere of activities is that of religious articles. These would be expected to remain Hispanic (Catholic) in symbolism and include such items as crucifixes, rosary beads, and religious medallions. An adoption of native religious articles and/or motifs (e.g., zemis) would perhaps be an indication of an ideological shift and prompt a reassessment of the hypothesis.

3. Structures at Puerto Real should employ local materials in their construction; however, the architectural style and physical layout of the town should be Hispanic in nature. Specifically this would involve rectangular single family houses with fenced or walled yards (Manucy 1978) laid out in a grid pattern around a central plaza. The Taino houses and towns were very different. The average Taino house or *bohio* was circular and housed several families (Rouse 1948:525). It was made of cane, plastered with mud, and surmounted by a straw roof (Oviedo 1959:39). The towns varied in size from 1 to 1,000 such houses, irregularly arranged and having one or more ball courts (Rouse 1948:524).

This implication follows from the hypothesized Spanish affiliation in visible areas of colonial culture, and also from the explicit norms and guidelines for spatial patterns established in sixteenth-century Spain to guide New World town planning (Crouch et al. 1982). Although these ordinances were not established until the latter half of the sixteenth century, the principles behind them were in effect from the time of initial conquest in 1492 (Foster 1960:49). It is interesting to note that this was a new idea being tested by Spain as a "directed change." Towns already established there were not uniformly laid out (Foster 1960:16). The limited amount of excavation conducted at Puerto Real does not allow for a detailed description of structure type and town layout. However, enough was uncovered to satisfy the test implication.

4. The diet of the colonist should show a mixture of the Iberian barnyard complex of peninsular Spain and the mixed hunting-farming strategies of the indigenous peoples. This pattern of food-ways, identified in St. Augustine (Reitz and Cumbaa 1983), was a modification of the traditional foodways in response to a new environment. According to Reitz and Cumbaa (1983:155–56), if the Iberian complex was transferred intact, then the New World faunal assemblage would consist primarily of sheep, cattle, and hogs, in that order. The diet would also have included domestic fowl, fish but few wild mammals.

To hypothesize that this complex would have survived, intact, is unrealistic because it is documented that sheep did not prosper on the islands. Also inasmuch as meals were, in many cases, prepared by native wives or servants, the incorporation of local wild species into the Spanish colonial diet would be expected. Reitz and Scarry (1985:99), on the basis of further research in St. Augustine, have refined the hypothesized colonial subsistence strategy to seven key responses to the New World environment:

1) they abandoned traditional resources unsuited to the new environment; 2) they adopted a new constellation of domestic plant resources; 3) they incorporated aboriginal patterns of wild fauna exploitation; 4) they retained Old World cultigens, primarily fruits, which could be grown locally; 5) they husbanded those Old World domestic animals which could survive with limited attention in the local conditions; 6) they added a few exotic New World cultigens to the locally grown plants; 7) they relied to a limited extent on imported foodstuffs.

A good faunal sample from Locus 19 and other loci at Puerto Real has been recovered that allows comments on the carniverous side of the colonial diet to be made. Additionally, there is good faunal data from the nearby Taino site at En Bas Saline that can be used for comparative purposes.

5. The material and faunal assemblage should reflect a crystallization of the proposed Hispanic-American colonial pattern through time. It is expected that as the colonists became more specifically adapted to the New World physical and social environment,

their methods of coping would become standardized. This patterned behavior should be reflected in the archaeological assemblage in such areas as foodways, architecture, and status artifacts. Variations among households from this predicted pattern should become less evident in later periods.

A key issue in this regard is the duration of occupation at Puerto Real, which amounted to approximately seventy-five years. Is this long enough to detect a crystallization of the Spanish colonial pattern? It is possible to clearly distinguish between late and early occupation at Puerto Real?

In the latter case, the answer is yes. As will be discussed later, it was possible, using stratigraphy and artifact *terminus post quems* to distinguish the Early Period (pre-1550) from the Late Period (post-1550) occupation. The date 1550 was chosen as the dividing point because it was roughly midway through the occupation of the town and because several types of ceramics are known to have been unavailable before this date and can be used as temporal markers.

The question of when crystallization occurred is impossible to pinpoint. Culture change is a dynamic process and any divisions imposed are artificial. This does not invalidate the study of culture crystallization as a process. Some crystallization would be expected after five years. Deagan (1983) described the Spanish colonial pattern using data from the eighteenth century, 200 years after settlement. It will be interesting to note what changes there are in the material assemblage after only a relatively short period of time.

The above five test implications provided the framework that guided the recovery and interpretation of the data from Puerto Real, and provide a means of assessing the utility of the working hypothesis. What is being specifically asked of the data is: "How do we characterize the changes that happened to the Iberian culture of the colonists?" The task, then, at Puerto Real is to identify patterns in the material culture that reflect the changes that the Spaniards underwent en route to becoming *creoles*.

5

Strategy and Tactics

The purpose of the 1984–85 fieldwork at Puerto Real was to identify patterns in the material culture that reflect the creolization of
the colonists' culture. This was done by testing implications arising
from the hypothesized pattern of Spanish colonial adaptation (see
chapter 1) identified in St. Augustine, Florida, by Deagan (1983).
Archaeological testing of this hypothesis required the extensive excavation of a Spanish colonial habitation outside of St. Augustine.
The site of Puerto Real fulfilled the requirements of the proposed
test.

The project was conducted over two ten-week periods during the
summers of 1984 and 1985. Excavations were conducted by the
author, a field assistant, a field laboratory supervisor, and a crew of
between twelve and fifteen Haitians. Based on the 1982 survey of
the site, a suitable area was selected and excavated. A brief re-
capitulation of the 1982 survey will illustrate its pivotal role in se-
lecting the locus of excavation.

The 1982 field season complemented previous work at Puerto
Real by establishing the town boundaries and completing a program of systematic subsurface sampling and topographic mapping
over the entire site (Williams 1986). Material recovered from the
tests was quantified and the data entered into the mainframe computer at the University of Florida. Using the SYMAP graphics program, several maps were prepared that portrayed the subsurface
distribution of various types of artifacts throughout the site. By

49

Figure 5.1. Masonry Loci at Puerto Real (*Williams 1986, reprinted with permission*)

mapping the distribution of masonry debris, it was possible to discern the locations of masonry structures. Fifty-seven structural areas were defined and could be categorized according to the abundance and diversity of Spanish and non-Spanish artifacts associated with them (figure 5.1). These groups are believed to represent different social and economic components of the community and are interpreted by reference to the documentarily verified archaeological patterns of Spanish St. Augustine (Deagan 1983).

Using the computer-generated maps, a suitable area was selected for excavation. Of the fifty-seven possible structural areas defined by Williams (1986), Locus 19 (Figure 5.2) seemed the most likely to provide the information sought. The abundance of masonry debris indicated the presence of a structure and the volume and type of ceramics in this locus suggested a high-status occupation dating to the second half of the sixteenth century. This would permit diachronic comparisons with Loci 33 and 35, an early sixteenth-century, high-status household, while controlling for economic status.

In addition to the SYMAP, reference was made to the contour map prepared by previous crews. The areas outlined by the SYMAP were a good guide, but still could only localize the suspected structures to within a half-acre area. The contour maps permitted a better on-site orientation for the author as well as delineating promising, yet subtle, topographic features.

The grid system employed at Locus 19 was merely an extension of that established by Willis in 1980. He had also placed concrete markers at 80 m intervals on the grid. Although some of these markers had been dislodged by local farmers who had tethered their cattle to them, enough remained in place so that the grid could be reestablished.

A transit station was set up to ensure vertical control of the units. The excavation units themselves measured 1.5 x 2.0 m and were excavated in arbitrary levels of 10 cm. The original intention had been to excavate by natural levels as had been done on previous projects (McEwan 1983, Willis 1984). However, very little soil differentiation was apparent at Locus 19. Natural stratigraphy consisted of a thin humus layer overlying a homogenous clay/loam which, itself, surmounted a sterile clay subsoil. The extremely arid conditions, which rapidly dried out the soil despite the use of

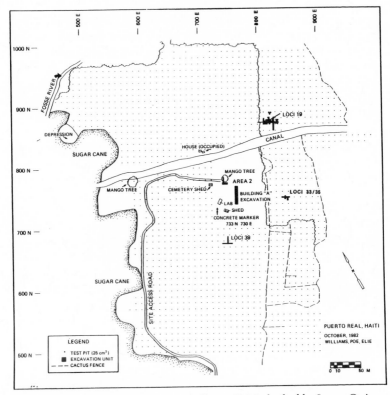

Figure 5.2. Location of Locus 19 *(Williams 1986, drafted by James Quine, reprinted with permission)*

garden sprayers and sun shades, did not make the job of distinguishing natural levels any easier. By excavating in 10 cm increments it was possible to differentiate between early and late occupations of the locus on the basis of datable artifacts.

All excavated soil was passed through one-quarter inch hardware cloth attached to a rigid frame. It was not possible to water screen due to the extreme scarcity of water at the site. Water for use in the lab and on the site had to be hauled by bucket from a well several hundred yards away. However, the Haitian workers were exceptionally perceptive and often found the tiniest artifacts (e.g., straight pins, seed beads) in situ. A point system for artifacts, devised by the workers, provided a spirit of friendly competition and boosted artifact recovery. The workers at the screen were also adept at spotting small artifacts. In addition, soil samples were taken of all discrete areas and features.

A field lab was set up on the site for preliminary processing of all recovered material before shipment to the United States. All excavated material was sent to the lab, where it was rough sorted into four main categories: artifacts, fauna, brick, and stone. The artifacts and faunal material were washed and air-dried on racks made especially for that purpose. The brick and stone was weighed and discarded. This was done because weight and provenience were all that was necessary to determine density and distribution of building rubble. Besides, the cost of transporting several tons of rubble to the United States was prohibitive and the logistics impossible. However, any brick that retained any two of three measurable dimensions (height, width, and length) was saved. The same is true of any piece of masonry that was at all unusual (e.g., maker's mark and glazing). All artifacts were shipped to the Florida State Museum, where they underwent additional analysis.

Fieldwork in 1984 was particularly challenging in that the author had never been to Haiti before, let alone visited the site. Assisting him in the field was fellow graduate student Greg Smith. Tim Deagan, a recent graduate of Florida State University, was in charge of setting up and running the field laboratory. The buildings, a storage shed and lab shed, built in 1979 during Willis's project, were found to be in good general repair. Unfortunately, just after the close of the 1985 field season, a freak windstorm was to destroy the lab shed.

Shortly after the team's arrival at the site, local villagers and farmers, who had worked for past projects, arrived to inquire about employment with the current project. In a difficult decision, thirteen men out of many applicants were hired and the crew put to work immediately clearing the area to be excavated. The area was not currently under cultivation but was covered by tall grass and low thorny trees known as baya hondas. Several days were required to clear the area using machetes.

It was decided to place the initial excavations, on a low rise of ground, in the middle of the masonry concentration as depicted on the SYMAP. Excavation confirmed the prediction that Locus 19 was primarily a high-status, Late-Period occupation. A total of twenty-five 1.5 x 2.0 m excavation units were excavated to sterile subsoil in 10 cm levels. All digging was done by trowel because it proved most suitable for the recovery of small fragile artifacts and was more efficient than a shovel for removal of the hard, baked clay/loam soil. The Haitians were also very adept at the use of the trowel due to previous experience on the other projects. Another tool used with great effect was the *luchette*. This locally made tool was essentially a five-foot chisel and was used to break up the hard clay. To minimize the dessicating effects of the sun, shades were constructed. They consisted of a wooden frame covered by a nylon parachute (purchased cheaply as surplus property) of a size just large enough to cover an individual unit. These sun shades were lightweight, portable, and functioned well for the season, though a couple were lost to freakish wind gusts.

Excavations in 1984 yielded more than 29,000 artifacts and 335 kg of faunal material from an extensive midden deposit. The artifacts, which will be described in more detail later, included a wide array of sixteenth-century Spanish material highlighted by some unique and interesting items. A small, gilded, unicorn pendant was recovered along with forty-six copper maravedis and an abundance or ornate Venetian *latticinio*-decorated glass. A couple of intricately worked brass and enamel book clasps were also found. Frustratingly, although a phenomenal amount of sixteenth-century refuse had been unearthed, the house associated with the midden eluded detection for most of the field season.

Finally, five test trenches were excavated in an effort to locate the structure. As is so often the case in archaeology, the structure was discovered during the last week of the 1984 field season, under a large pile of backdirt. The excavation strategy immediately changed in response to the discovery. All work on the exploratory trenches ceased, and the efforts of the entire crew were brought to bear on exposing as much of the foundation as possible in the time remaining. Heroic efforts exposed 8 m of the wall, but no corner was found.

The foundation consisted of a paired row of large rocks, on the top of which rested smaller stones (figure 5.3). On the final day of

Figure 5.3. Wall Foundation at Locus 19 (*photo by author*)

Figure 5.4. Brick Drain (photo by author)

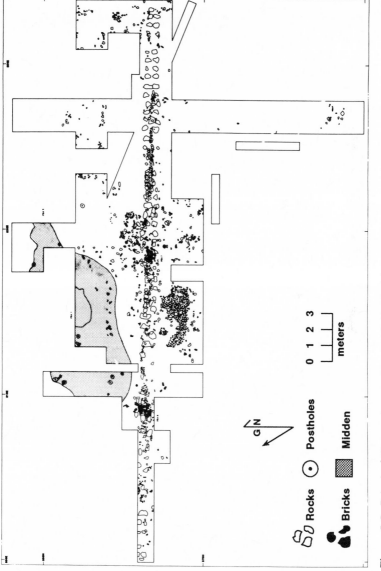

Figure 5.5. Principal Excavations at Locus 19 *(drafted by author)*

fieldwork, plastic sheeting was placed over the in situ foundation stones and the site was backfilled. The location of the foundation was carefully noted and corner stakes to the units were pounded flush with the ground to aid in locating the area the following year.

The 1985 field season picked up where the previous season left off, with some exceptions. Assisting in the field was Patty Peacher and supervising the lab was James Cusick, both new graduate students at the University of Florida. The Haitian crew, which had performed admirably in the field the previous season, was rehired virtually intact.

The complete excavation of the foundation was the primary objective of the 1985 season. Excavation units were put in to follow the wall to the corners. The wall extended for a distance of over 20 m and had two brick drains set in the western section (figure 5.4). The length of the wall surprised everyone, including the Haitian workers, who claimed that it "extended all the way to Santo Domingo." A cross trench, 22 m in length, was placed midway along the foundation in an effort to locate the opposite wall of the structure. The wall was not found using this technique.

At the end of the 1985 season, a total of forty-six 2 x 2 m units had been excavated (figure 5.5). These excavations yielded 20,367 artifacts and approximately 146 kg of faunal material. Over 500 kg of brick and stone rubble had been weighed and discarded at the lab. Fewer artifacts and fauna were recovered during the 1985 project because of the location of the excavation units outside of the midden. The 1985 project concentrated on the structure itself and not its midden as had occurred during the previous season.

6

Excavated Data

This chapter discusses the artifacts recovered from Locus 19. These data will be presented with a minimum of interpretation because the purpose of this chapter is to provide a descriptive artifact guide to be used for reference purposes. The author's interpretations, as applied to the research questions, are presented in the following chapter.

Puerto Real is an extremely rich site. During the century following its abandonment, French planters robbed the buildings of most of their brick and stone but not, apparently, of their refuse. With the aboveground portion of the town removed, the site was quickly forgotten. Subsequent inhabitants did little to disturb the site. The local Haitian villagers practice only hoe horticulture. Thus, the material assemblage associated with Puerto Real shows little evidence of disturbance.

During the 1984–85 field season more than 49,000 artifacts were recovered. The material assemblage was organized into functionally specific groups for analytic and comparative purposes. These categories were first proposed by South (1977:92) and have been modified for work on Spanish colonial sites (table 6.1). The purpose of these groups is to provide a meaningful organization of the artifact assemblage in terms of human behavior as well as a basis for inter- and intra-site comparison. Particular attention has been given to the ceramic assemblage because it has been demonstrated at St. Augustine to provide a chronological framework for assessing change, as well as an index for measuring status differences within the community (Deagan 1983:231–62).

The faunal assemblage was as extensive as that of the artifacts. The sheer bulk of the fauna (more than 480 kg) made a complete faunal analysis impractical given the time and financial constraints. A representative sample was selected that included all the fauna from the major features as well as some from the zone deposition.

The artifacts recovered will be described, both qualitatively and quantitatively, sequentially according to group number. An exception will be made in the case of Group 20, Hispanic tablewares (non-majolica), in order to keep the ceramics together as a group. Appendix 1 consists of a table denoting the distribution of the types of artifacts within each group.

After analysis of their artifacts, the proveniences were assigned to either the Early or Late Period of occupation. The period proveniences were distinguished by stratigraphic position and the presence of such ceramics as Orange micaceous ware, Ming porcelain, and Cologne stoneware, all of which are characterized by previous research as having a *terminus post quem* of 1550. Proveniences in the earlier time periods were distinguished both stratigraphically and by the absence of any late ceramic time markers. The data recovered from the excavations revealed that levels 1 and 2 were relatively undisturbed by post-sixteenth-century activity and could be dated to the Late Period of occupation of the town. Level 3 was a transitional strata between the Early and Late Periods, and level 4 appeared to date to the pre-1550 occupation of Puerto Real.

Each artifact will be described according to its composition, decoration, form, and chronological placement (if known). Nonclassified types will be carefully described and illustrated whenever possible. The primary references used for identifying the ceramics were: the comparative collection of the Florida State Museum, Deagan (1987), Goggin (1968), and Lister and Lister (1982).

Group 1 - Majolica

Bisque. Although specimens of Bizcocho, a thin, unglazed, non-utilitarian ware, have been found at Puerto Real (Hodges Collec-

Table 6.1 Artifact Categories at Puerto Real

Group	Artifacts
1	Majolica
2	European Utilitarian Ceramics
3	Non-Majolica European Tablewares
4	Colono and Aboriginal Ceramics
5	Kitchen Artifacts
6	Structural Hardware
7	Weaponry and Armor
8	Clothing and Sewing Items
9	Personal Items and Jewelry
10	Activity-Related Items
11	Unidentified Metal Objects
12	Masonry Construction Items
13	Furniture Hardware
14	Tools
15	Toys and Games
16	Harness and Tack
17	Religious Items
18	Miscellaneous Substances
19	Unaffiliated Artifacts
20	Hispanic Tablewares

tion, Limbe, Haiti), ceramics in this category primarily refer to majolica fragments that have lost their glaze. For this reason they were included here. Most specimens were extremely small.

Caparra Blue. Named for the site of Caparra, Puerto Rico, Caparra Blue is a distinctive two-tone majolica. The exterior is a solid, dark-blue enamel, and the interior is white or off-white. Some of the specimens from Puerto Real have a slight greenish cast to the interior white enamel. Deagan (1987) suggests that these may have been produced at Panama Vieja in the late sixteenth century. This type is known only in the *albarelo*, or drug-jar form, and dates to the sixteenth century (Goggin 1968:134–35).

Columbia Plain. This type was easily the most numerous majolica type at Puerto Real. It accounts for more than 80 percent of all the majolicas recovered from the site. This was also the most variable types in the assemblage. The glaze ranged from a thick, glossy, opaque white to a thin, matte, pinkish off-white. The paste was uniformly chalky in consistency but varied in color from terra cotta to cream. Several vessel forms were noted. Most numerous among these were *escudillas* and simple *platos* (see figure 6.1). However, such forms as *pichels, jarros,* and porringers were also found (figure 6.2).

Several pieces had been identified as a variant known as Columbia Plain Gunmetal, described as having a "darkened, rather than white ground [that] . . . varies from a dense irridescent black to a light specked grey" (Lister and Lister 1982:48). Recent research has shown that this is probably due to post-deposition discoloration (Deagan 1987). Another variant found at Puerto Real that is, in fact, real is Columbia Plain Green. This variant makes up 2 percent of the majolica assemblage and is simply a Columbia Plain vessel that has been partially covered with a clear, green glaze. This is an early variant dating to the first half of the sixteenth century (Goggin 1968:118).

An interesting phenomenon noticed on several of the Columbia Plain specimens was the presence of marks that had been scratched through the glaze of the finished vessel (figure 6.3). Goggin (1968:119) noticed this on sherds from the Convento de San Francisco at Santo Domingo and attributed them to property marks put on by the owners rather than the makers.

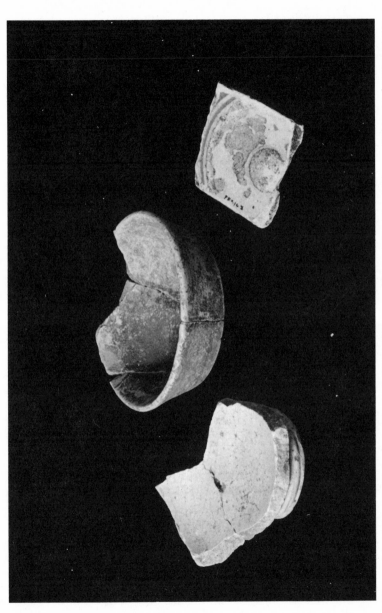

Figure 6.1. Columbia Plain *Escudillas* (left FS# 3342, center FS# 3182); Yayal Blue on White (right FS# 3168) *(photo by James Quine; Florida Museum of Natural History Collection)*

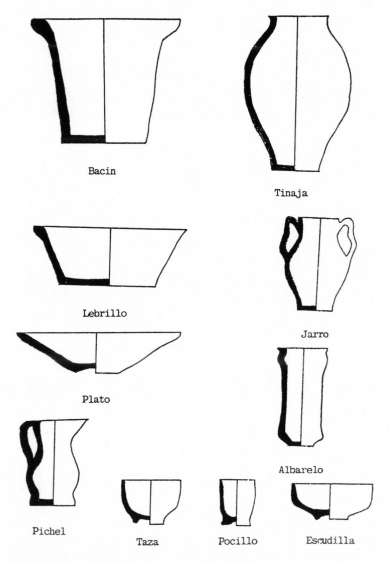

Figure 6.2. Vessel Forms *(adapted from Deagan, 1987)*

Figure 6.3. Owners' Marks on Ceramics: A—FS# 3281; B—FS# 3165; C—FS# 3159; D—FS# 3395; E—FS# 3310; F—FS# 3343, Isabela Polychrome fragment; G—FS# 3292 *(photo by James Quine; Florida Museum of Natural History Collection)*

Cuenca Tile. Only one fragment of Cuenca tile was recovered from Locus 19, though more than a dozen were found at Building A (Willis 1984:213). All the tiles corresponded to Goggin's type B. This type features floral motifs deeply stamped onto the surface and colored with blue, green, honey-colored brown, and manganese. This type dates to the sixteenth century (Goggin 1968:145–46).

Lusterware. Also known as *Reflejo Metalico*, this interesting type is represented by a single sherd at Locus 19, and is rare in New World contexts in general. It is characterized by a design of a reflective, iridescent luster of copper-gold on an off-white base (Deagan 1987:38).

Isabela Polychrome. A dozen pieces of Isabela Polychrome were recovered from Locus 19. All were *plato* forms, including one large rim fragment. This type has a Columbia Plain type paste and a dull blue and manganese purple design on an off-white enamel surface. Designs are concentric lines of blue surrounding a band of purple or stylized *alafias* (Goggin 1968:126–27). The time range of this type appears to be the first three-quarters of the sixteenth century (Deagan 1987).

La Vega Blue on White. This is a very poorly known type. Only three sherds were recovered and their identification is uncertain. Goggin (1968:130–31) defines it as crude, simple floral motifs executed in blue on a Columbia Plain base. This type of majolica is mostly found in *plato* form. Deagan (1987) points out that the type fragments are small and may actually be from Yayal blue on white vessels having central designs.

Ligurian Blue on Blue. A minor type at Locus 19, Ligurian Blue on Blue, was originally called Ichtucknee Blue on Blue by Goggin (1968:135). Ichtucknee Blue on Blue was later divided into Ligurian Blue on Blue and Sevilla Blue on Blue. The former is "a thin, delicate, blue ground ware carrying fine darker blue patterns, occasionally brightened by a patch of yellow or a bit of white" (Lister and Lister 1984:72). This type is solidly dated to the second half of the sixteenth century (Deagan 1987). The specimens recovered at Locus 19 were small fragments of *plato* and small bowl or cup forms.

Montelupo Polychrome. This was represented at Locus 19 by the most common of its three varieties. It "has a light cream-colored paste and thick, rather heavy vessel bodies . . . [and] exhibits a design of geometric bands in orange, yellow, blue, and black-outlines yellow" (Deagan 1987). Although not numerous, Montelupo polychrome is not uncommon at Puerto Real, having been found on the surface (Hodges Collection) and at Building A (Willis 1984:158). This type dates to the first half of the sixteenth century (Lister and Lister 1984:72).

Sevilla Blue on Blue. Formerly included in the category Ichtucknee Blue on Blue, this type is a Sevillian form inspired by the Italianate Ligurian Blue on Blue. It is characterized by broad, heavy-stroked patterns of dark blue on a lighter blue background. Poorly represented at Locus 19, it has a TPQ of 1550 (Deagan 1987).

Sevilla Blue on White. A recently defined type (Lister and Lister 1982:60), this majolica is represented by only a single dubious sherd at Puerto Real. It is characterized by a clear cobalt-blue design on Sevilla White vessels, and the chronological range is from about 1530 to 1650 (Deagan 1987).

Santo Domingo Blue on White. This is a decorated type of common-grade Morisco Ware that was common throughout the sixteenth century. The blue design motifs are described as "a hodgepodge of broad sweeping lines, dashes, random dots, squiggles, and lobed and wavy lines" (Lister and Lister 1982:57). The forms excavated at Puerto Real were *platos* and *escudillas*.

Yayal Blue on White. Fairly common at Locus 19, this type is represented by seventy sherds. It is another type that has a Columbia Plain-like paste, enamel, and surface finish. Its simple design elements consist of blue bands in concentric circles on the interior of the vessel. A crude central medallion design is sometimes also included (Deagan 1987). The *plato* form was most common at Locus 19, though some *escudilla* fragments were noted.

White Majolica. This category consists mainly of small fragments of majolica. It was difficult to assign them to any plain majolica type (e.g., Sevilla White or Faenza White) because the possibility exists that the small specimens were simply a plain fragment from a blue on white or polychrome vessel.

UID Majolica. Next to Columbia Plain, this was the most numerous category, accounting for 5 percent of all majolicas. This category includes blue on white, blue on blue, and polychrome majolicas that could not be identified at the present time.

Santa Elena Green and White. Common at Locus 19, this type has been identified at the site of Santa Elena, in South Carolina, and appears to date to the second half of the sixteenth century. It is described as a "highbread [*sic*] majolica with a green lead-glazed exterior and a white tin glazed interior" (Skowronek 1987:8). Lesser forms at Locus 19 seem to be large bowls.

Puerto Real Green and Green. This majolica warrants a new type designation. Vessels of this type are thick-bodied and have a pinkish paste with a dark-green, tin glazed exterior and a lighter olive-green, lead-glazed interior. Vessel forms appear to be large bowls.

Group 2 - Utilitarian Wares

This group of ceramics includes those types that, as the category title implies, are primarily functional rather than decorative. Utilitarian group ceramics serve as storage vessels and are used in food-preparation activities.

El Morro. First defined by Hale Smith (1962:68–69), this type was redefined by Deagan (1976), but the term seems to be used only by Florida-trained researchers, others referring to it as lead-glazed coarse earthenware. This thin, lead-glazed, coarse earthenware is distinctive in its poorly smoothed, granular surface (Deagan 1987). The glaze was often incompletely applied and "varies in color from a pale yellow-orange to a dark brown or olive green" (Willis 1976: 128). The limited use of the term El Morro for this ceramic makes the assignment of the chronological range difficult, though reports of the type span three centuries, from the sixteenth to the eighteenth century (Deagan 1987). Forms recovered from Puerto Real include *platos* and small bowls.

Green Bacin/Green Lebrillo. This type includes a variety of large utilitarian forms, of which the Bacin and Lebrillo are most common. It has paste close to majolica in texture, is covered with a heavy, clear, dark-green matte glaze, and seems confined to the sixteenth century in the Caribbean (Goggin 1968:226; Deagan 1987).

It is fairly common at Puerto Real and is represented at Locus 19 by more than 300 sherds, including several large basin rims.

Olive Jar. The most numerous of utilitarian ceramics at Locus 19, more than 8,000 sherds of olive jar were recovered, accounting for 63 percent of this category. The majority of the sherds recovered have been classified as early style. This style was defined by Goggin (1960:8–11) as having a distinctively shaped globular body; a raised, everted mouth; and attached handles. The exterior surface was often covered by a white slip, and the interior was often glazed in some shade of green. Goggin dates this style from 1493 to approximately 1575. The olive jar rims from Locus 19 are characteristically early style (figure 6.4) though two middle-style necks were recovered from Late Period proveniences. Skowronek (1987:12–13) indicates that the "middle style" olive jar may have been appearing as early as the mid-sixteenth century. The discovery of these middle-style sherds is important because it represents solid evidence that this type was appearing before its commonly supposed *terminus post quem.*

Glazed olive jar accounts for 23 percent of all olive jars at Locus 19. The color of this lead glaze was usually green or brownish-yellow. An interesting deviation from the usual glaze colors was the presence of twelve red-glazed olive jar fragments. This appeared to be the result of a clear lead glaze applied over a red slip because some unglazed red slipped olive jar fragments were also recovered. All but one of these sherds were found in Late Period proveniences.

Spanish Storage Jar. This type of ceramic is defined by vessel form rather than by characteristics of paste or surface treatment. It has an olive jar-type paste and has been identified in *jarro* and *bacin* forms (Deagan 1987). At Locus 19 this type is, no doubt, underrepresented because only flat-bottomed basal sherds could be confidently placed in this type. Like olive jar, Spanish storage jar also often had an interior green glaze.

Redware. A difficult ware to categorize, this type is found at Locus 19 in both utilitarian and special-function tableware forms. Deagan (1987:38) defines it as being characterized by an "orange or brick-red earthenware paste . . . uniform [in] color on both surfaces and through the core of the sherds." Forms recovered at Puerto Real varied from thick, large bowls to thin, delicate, small

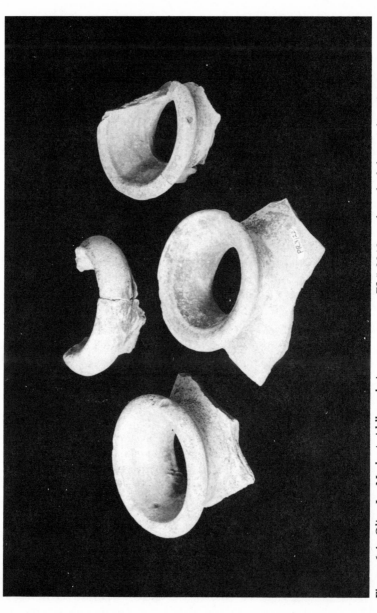

Figure 6.4. Olive Jar Necks (middle style in upper center, FS# 3312; early style, left to right: FS# 3138, 3122, 3343) *photo by James Quine; Florida Museum of Natural History Collection)*

jarros, pichels, and bowls. Several of the sherds were incised with wavy lines, which Deagan (1987) reports as being found on sixteenth-century specimens. It is difficult, at this time, to determine a time range or place of origin because the New World potters were turning out redwares by the late sixteenth century (Deagan 1987) and production continued through the eighteenth century.

Unidentified Coarse Earthenwares. A great many sherds (30 percent) could not be identified any further than this general heading. Ceramics in this category have a soft, low-fired paste exhibiting high porosity (Deagan 1987). Specimens were sometimes lead-glazed with honey, brown, green, and red being the usual colors of the glaze. Vessel forms tended to overlap the tableware category, including *platos* and small bowls as well as large utilitarian vessels.

Group 3 - European Tablewares

This category of ceramics consists of tablewares of a non-Hispanic origin. Poorly represented, the entire category consists of only slightly more than 200 sherds, or less than 1 percent of the total ceramic assemblage. Considering that Puerto Real was dissolved because of its traffic with non-Hispanic smugglers, one might have expected that many of the smuggled goods were ceramics. This may not have been the case, Andrews (1978:182) states that textiles were the chief trade item of the French smugglers. Perhaps the other smugglers dealt primarily in perishables as well.

Cologne Stoneware. This ware was named for the city in which these wares were produced (figure 6.5). This European ceramic is described as a "grey-bodied stoneware coated with an iron oxide slip that broke into a brown mottle when fired in a salt glaze kiln" (Noel-Hume 1970:55). According to Noel-Hume, the earliest examples date to 1550, so it is a good temporal marker at Locus 19.

Porcelain. Oriental porcelain was not available in the Caribbean until at least 1550 and then only through Portuguese corsairs. It was not until the Manila galleon trade in 1573 that Spain began supplying its colonies with Chinese porcelain (Deagan 1987). All

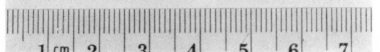

Figure 6.5. Cologne Stoneware, FS# 3401 *(photo by James Quine; Florida Museum of Natural History Collection)*

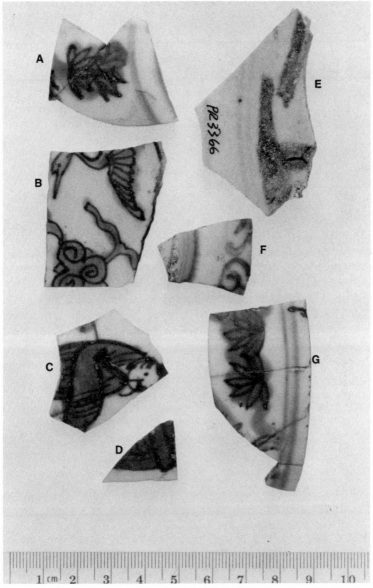

Figure 6.6. Ming Porcelain: A—FS# 3120; B—FS# 3340; C—FS# 3119; D—FS# 3120; E—FS# 3366; F—FS# 3367; G—FS# 3120 *(photo by James Quine; Florida Museum of Natural History Collection)*

sixteenth-century porcelains in the New World were produced during the Ming Dynasty (1522–1643) in China. Characteristic of this ware is "a rather unctuous glaze of a distinct bluish green tinge. Its decoration is . . . of a deep warm blue of violet tone" (Aga-Oglu 1956:92). Most of the sherds recovered at Puerto Real are from small bowls or cups (figure 6.6). Considering the difficulties a colonist must have had in obtaining the pieces there, a surprising amount of porcelain was recovered at Locus 19: 45 fragments. Because Puerto Real was abandoned a scant five years after the commencement of the Manila galleon trade, it seems likely that Portuguese smugglers were responsible for the relatively large quantity of porcelain scattered across Locus 19.

Non-Hispanic Tin-Enameled Wares. Very few of these wares have been recovered at Puerto Real, and these are small sherds. In England and the Netherlands, tin-enameled ceramics are known as Delft. Similarly, tin-enameled ceramics produced in France are known as Faience. Their identification at Puerto Real is difficult in that all comparative specimens dated to the sixteenth century or later. There are no contemporary French or English sites in the New World to compare with Puerto Real. Also, the fragments of these supposed non-Hispanic, tin-enameled wares were very fragmentary and lacked any design elements. For these reasons, the identification of Delft and/or Faience at Puerto Real is tentative.

Group 20 - Hispanic Tablewares (non-majolica)

Placed here for comparison with the rest of the ceramic assemblage, Group 20 includes those tablewares produced in Spain or its colonies that are not majolicas.

Feldspar-Inlaid Redware. First described by Charles Fairbanks (1966), this type is a typical thin redware decorated with white feldspar chips. This ware is common at Locus 19, consisting of more than 250 sherds. An interesting variant of this type is a feldspar-decorated type with a micaceous paste. Another variant is a feldspar-tempered ware of unknown form or function. Deagan (1987:43 suggests "that in the circum-Caribbean area Feldspar-Inlaid Redware dates from before 1550 until the end of the 16th century (ca. 1530–1600)." Vessel forms included small bowls.

Orange Micaceous Ware. This type accounts for 49 percent of the Group 20 assemblage (806 sherds). It has an orange paste with flecks of mica in the temper. Vessel forms are reported as generally small, in *taza, pocillo,* and *plato* forms (Deagan 1987). This is also the case at Locus 19.

Melado. This type has been called honey-colored/Seville ware (Willis 1984) and honey-colored ware (Goggin 1968, McEwan 1983). Deagan (1987) describes it as having a cream to terra cotta-colored paste covered with a honey-colored, opaque lead glaze. It is distinct from other similarly colored wares by its opacity and fine paste. Vessel forms at Locus 19 are generally *platos* and *escudillas.* Goggin (1968:227) places the chronological range of this ceramic between 1493 and 1550.

Group 4 - Colono and Aboriginal Ceramics

Descriptions of the ceramics in this category are taken fom Greg Smith (1986:49–55). His thesis represents the definitive work on non-European coarse earthenwares at Locus 19.

Meillac. This is an aboriginal form characterized by fine-grained temper, relatively thin walls (3–7 mm), and a polished gray or red surface. Designs, when present, include incised cross-hatching and oblique parallel lines; vessel forms are usually round or boat-shaped bowls.

Carrier. This is another aboriginal type generally thought to postdate Meillac, though the Puerto Real research suggests some degree of both prehistoric and historic overlap between the two types. Carrier has coarser temper, thicker walls (7–9 mm), and a more highly polished grayish-brown surface. Incised designs are commonly curved and often end with circular punctuations. Adornos (bat-shaped forms are common) are often applied to the shoulders of the bowl or jar forms.

Christophe Plain. These simple, bowl-shaped ceramics were previously referred to as Colono ware (Willis 1984) because they resembled neither Meillac or Carrier ceramics (figure 6.7). Willis (1984:169) used the term Colono ware to "designate its supposed

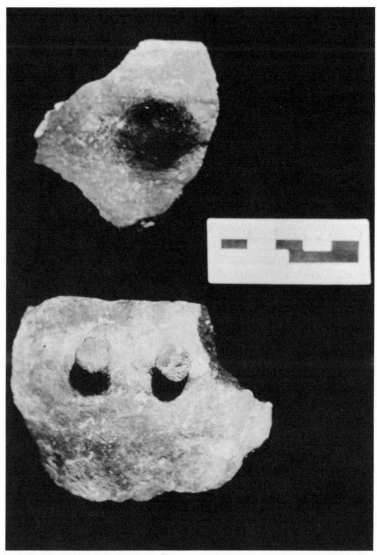

Figure 6.7. Christophe Plain *(photo by James Quine; Florida Museum of Natural History Collection)*

hybrid property, the result of European contact with aboriginal populations. . . . In addition to this Colono-Indian hybrid, several authors, most notably Leland Ferguson (1978:14–28), have suggested the possibility of a second hybrid type resulting from the European-African slave contact situation."

Greg Smith defines this new type as "measuring up to 19 mm in thickness, with a paste characterized by abundant quartzite inclusions of up to 1 cm in diameter, the function of these bowls appears to have been that of a cooking pot, since a large percentage of the sherds are sooted" (1986:54).

Red Slipped. Greg Smith (1986) distinguishes between two types of red-slipped pottery at Puerto Real. One type is extremely rare, and the other is far more numerous and increased in popularity through time. The cultural affiliation of the first type is definitely aboriginal; that of the second, is uncertain, though Smith suspects it is European. He describes this type as "thin walled (3–6 mm) and well-smoothed, with a very fine-grained texture. Vessels appear in small jar and/or bottle forms and show no signs of having been made on a wheel" (1986:55). More formal analysis (e.g., compositional) is necessary to determine where these wares originated. Of the red-slipped pottery recovered, the vast majority are of the second type.

Unidentified Plain Pottery. Plain group 4 ceramics that did not fit in the above classifications were put into this category. The rationale behind this category was to "avoid the error of assuming that all 'non-traditional' Meillac and Carrier sherds were Christophe Plain" (Greg Smith 1986:55).

Unidentified Decorated Ware. A relatively uncommon type, these ceramics possess design elements distinct from Meillac or Carrier types.

Group 5 - Kitchen Artifacts

As the title suggests, items in this group are associated with food handling, preparation, or consumption activities. Included are all glass except window glass and those types of glass associated with personal possessions (i.e., perfume bottles and watch crystals). All tablewares except ceramics, which are grouped separately, are in this category.

Glass. Glass of all types was very common at Locus 19, totaling well over 1,000 fragments. A variety of vessel forms is represented, most of which are generally small and delicate bottles, decanters (three glass stoppers were recovered), and vials, though stemmed goblets are present. Although most of the glass recovered was clear, a variety of colors were found as well, including aqua, blue, several shades of green, purple, opaque red, yellow, and polychrome. The polychrome pieces are an aesthetically pleasing swirl of red and blue. The glassware was often molded into different decorative shapes and some had small glass appliqués. Some of the clear glass had been etched, but the fragments were too small to discern the nature of the design. Barber (1917:5) claims that etched glass was of Italian origin or influence. The most decorative of the glassware is, undoubtedly, the delicate Italian *latticinio*-decorated glass (1917:6). Two varieties are present at Locus 19: clear with opaque, white ribbon stripes; and navy blue with white ribbon stripes (figure 6.8).

Knives. Two general types of iron knives were recovered from Locus 19: a sharp carving knife with a riveted bone or wood handle; and a one-piece, blunt-end table knife.

Non-Hispanic Items. Three unusual items in this group's assemblage are a stone metate fragment and two manos. These items were most likely used for the processing of maize into flour. The natives of Hispaniola primarily boiled their corn so would not have used manos or metates for this purpose. The presence of these artifacts suggests a local trade with the mainland. Wheat did not grow well on the islands, and cassava was used to feed the slaves and as a ship's store, but was not well liked by the colonists (Ewen 1985). Corn was an acceptable substitute and available from the mainland. The presence of thirty-one fragments of ceramic cassava griddle, discussed by Greg Smith (1986:55), suggests that cassava was being consumed by *someone* at Locus 19.

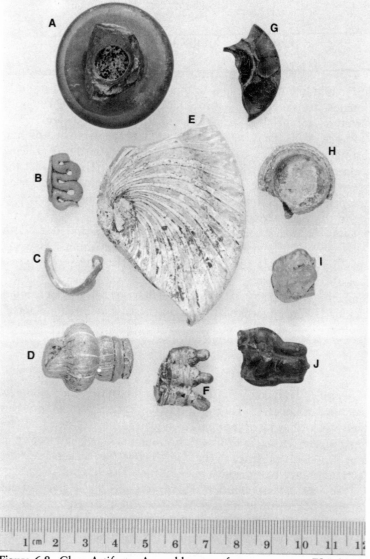

Figure 6.8. Glass Artifacts: A—goblet stem fragment, green, FS# 3113; B—looped appliqué, clear, FS# 3290; C—handle fragment, clear, FS# 3108; D—goblet stem fragment, clear, white stripes, FS# 3189; E—goblet base, clear, white stripes, FS# 3126; F—gilt-edged appliqué, heavily patinated, FS# 3299; G—base fragment, red and white mottled, FS# 3226; H—vial base (?), clear, white stripes, FS# 3132; I—rose-shaped appliqué, clear, white stripes, FS# 3289; J—handle fragment, red, FS# 3341 *(photo by James Quine; Florida Museum of Natural History Collection)*

Group 6 - Structural Hardware

This category consists of artifacts associated with standing structures. Window glass belongs in this group as opposed to group 5 (kitchen items). Note that brass tacks, associated primarily with furniture, are included with group 13 (furniture hardware).

Spikes, Nails, and Tacks. These artifacts are wrought iron and distinguished on the basis of length. A spike is defined here as being 8 cm or more in length; a tack, less than 2 cm. The fact that the overwhelming number of these artifacts were found in Late Period proveniences lends further credence to the idea of the structure dating to this time period.

Door Hardware. These items consisted of hinges and locks. Both locks were of iron and in a poor state of preservation. One specimen did preserve its outside, boxlike form. The hinges were of two types: staple and strap. The staple hinges were called cotter-key hinges by Willis (1984:181), which he described as a "simple interlocking U-Hinge mechanism used on chests, windows, or doors."

Group 7 - Weaponry and Armor

Armor. Two types of personal body armor have been tentatively identified at Locus 19. Three pieces of plate armor were found. This type was formed by overlapping iron plates attached to an underlying garment (Ffoulkes 1967:49). Five interlocking small iron rings may denote the presence of chain mail. However, the remains were so fragmentary that positive identification was not possible.

Weapons and Ammunition. There were very few artifacts in this category. Three small musket balls (varying between 1.2 and 1.7 cm in diameter) and one piece of lead shot were recovered. A possible iron spear point was identified that appears to have been reworked to form a pointed blade by hammering out the blade of a tanged file or rasp.

Figure 6.9. Bone Artifacts (right FS# 3291, lace bobbin; top left FS# 3334, carved bone; bottom left FS# 3125, carved bone) *(photo by James Quine; Florida Museum of Natural History Collection)*

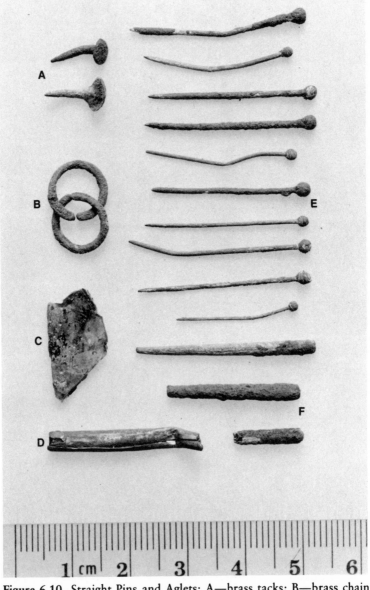

Figure 6.10. Straight Pins and Aglets: A—brass tacks; B—brass chain links; C—brass sheet fragment; D—silver aglet; E—brass straight pins; F—brass aglets *(photo by James Quine; Florida Museum of Natural History Collection)*

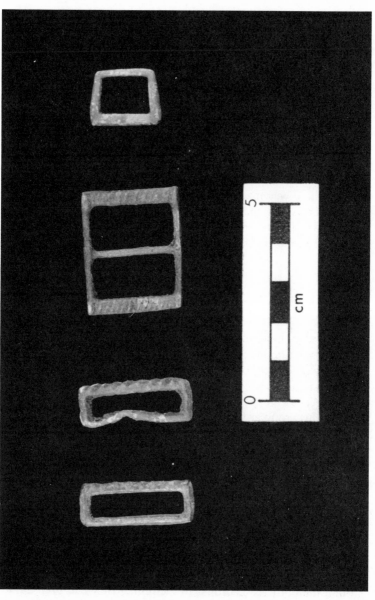

Figure 6.11. Brass Buckles (left to right: FS# 3132, 3339, 3333, 3356) *(photo by James Quine; Florida Museum of Natural History Collection)*

Group 8 - Clothing and Sewing Items

Sewing Items. Many metal artifacts associated with sewing were recovered at Locus 19. The most numerous were brass straight pins (figure 6.10). Other items include the remains of two pair of scissors, three thimbles, and a carved bone lace bobbin (figure 6.9).

Clothing Items. Like many of today's fashions, the clothing of the sixteenth century consisted mainly of cloth and other materials that do not preserve well over time. What *do* survive are the metallic artifacts that are functional or decorative accessories to clothing. Most prevalent at Locus 19 were aglets (copper alloy lacing tips). One of these was made of silver (figure 6.10). Less common fasteners were small shank buttons (made of pewter or silver) and hook-and-eye fasteners. A variety of brass and iron buckle types were also found (figure 6.11).

Group 9 - Personal Items

Artifacts included in this category are those that, in a systemic context, are usually associated with an individual: that is, items persons would carry on a regular basis, or that others would identify with that particular person.

Coins. These copper pieces were by far the most numerous artifact in this group at Locus 19 and, indeed, ubiquitous throughout the site of Puerto Real (figure 6.12). Most of the coins were in a very poor state of preservation. However, on the basis of size, it is believed that at least two denominations were present: four-maravedi and two-maravedi pieces. Of these, only the larger, the four-maravedi type, or cuarto, could be identified with any certainty. These are of the so-called "Santo Domingo type" and described by Adams (1974:492) as having a stylized "Y" in the center of the obverse with an "F" to the left and a "IIII" or "4" to the right. Around the border is "KAROLVS ET IONNA." On the reverse are pillars, flanked by "S" and "P" and "HISPANIARVM ET INDIA" around the border. According to Nesmith, "they had been authorized for the island by Ferdinand on December 20, 1505, and again

Obverse   Reverse

Figure 6.12. Four-maravedi coins *(photo by author; drawing adapted from Hodges, 1980)*

by Johanna on May 10, 1531. They were struck under contract at the mint of Seville or of Burgos, possibly at both" (1955:40).

Adams identifies two major types of these pieces that he distinguishes on the basis of whether the number "four" on the obverse was in Arabic or Roman numerals. He states (1974:493):

> Whether the first design bore the denomination in Roman numerals or Arabic figures there does not seem to be any way of discovering, but we may safely assume that these designs were in use from 1505 up to the time of law of July 16, 1695 when the design of the castles and lions was authorized.

Unfortunately, the collection from Puerto Real is of little help in clarifying this issue because only one coin with an Arabic numeral could be distinguished. It came from an early context. However, coins with Roman numerals were found in both early and late contexts. Again, it must be remembered that less than 10 percent of these coins had any visible surface features remaining.

Jewelry. Only small or broken fragments of jewelry were found. A piece of a jet ring was one of two such articles found at Locus 19. Interesting enough, jet rings were among the articles of jewelry owned by Charles V's mother, Joanna the Mad (Muller 1972:100). The other artifact was a very fine pendant that may have been part of a necklace (figure 6.13). Crafted into the shape of a unicorn, this item was made of brass or some other copper alloy and then covered with a layer of gold leaf. Muller (1972:27) states that zoomorphic forms were popular in pendants during the sixteenth century.

Beads. These are included in this category rather than in group 8 because they are large and probably functioned as jewelry. A variety of colors of beads of different manufacture and composition are represented at Locus 19. A representative sample are illustrated in figure 6.14 and will be described in detail on p. 89.

Figure 6.13. Unicorn Pendant (FS# 3148, 2 cm in length) *(photo by James Quine, Florida Museum of Natural History Collection)*

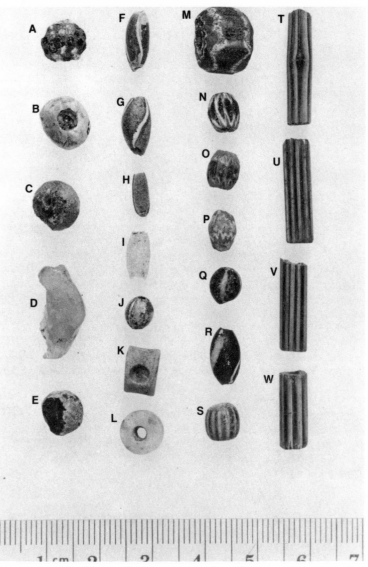

Figure 6.14. Bead Types from Locus 19: A—FS# 3305; B—3305; C—3138; D—3154; E—3165; F—3165; G—3302; H—3340; I—3293; J—3175; K—3377; L—3334; M—3385; N—3292; O—3323; P—3328; Q—3152; R—3299; S—3108; T—3403; U—3098; V—3369; W—3370. See p. 89 for description. *(photo by James Quine; Florida Museum of Natural History Collection)*

A—red glass "crumb" bead. Looking very much like a raspberry, this type of bead was manufactured by small spherical glass "crumbs" being applied to a larger, spherical glass core. This specimen is larger than the one illustrated as type #120 in Smith and Good (1982:43).

B & K—bone beads.

C & E—amber beads. These spherical beads are formed from fossilized tree resin, which is common in the Dominican Republic. Deagan (1987:181) dates these to the second half of the sixteenth century.

D—carnelian bead. A fragment of flat, diamond-shaped, orange carnelian, which had been biconically drilled. Although traded since Roman times, Deagan (1987:182) reports these as being most common on Spanish sites postdating the seventeenth century.

F, G & H—blue and white striped olive-shaped beads. G has alternating blue and white stripes with no visible core layer, and the stripes are not applied. F & H are four white and four blue stripes over a white core. These correspond to types 24–26 in Smith and Good (1982:41).

I—colorless olive-shaped bead with a large hole.

J, Q & R—tumbled blue/black bead with four white stripes.

L—white and green stone disk bead.

M, N, O & P—faceted chevron beads. Research performed by Smith and Good (1982:8) suggests that this type of bead is the "margarita" spoken of in Spanish documents. It is formed of alternating red, white, and blue layers of glass that are carved at the ends, exposing these layers. Deagan (1987:164–65) dates these to the sixteenth century. M & P correspond to type #82 (Smith and Good 1982:43). O corresponds to type #79 (1982:43). N was too weathered to make a determination.

S—tumbled chevron bead. Corresponds to type #123 in Smith and Good (1982:44).

T, U, V, W—striped cane chevron beads. Described in Smith and Good (1982:32) as a "tubular bead which appears blue and white striped: transparent light blue exterior that appears colorless except when held to the light/cobalt blue stripes inlaid between teeth of white layer/red/white/transparent light blue core." Corresponds to type #73.

I am indebted to Dr. Marvin Smith for identifying the above bead sample.

Book Hardware. Records hint that books may have been present at Puerto Real. Lyon (1981:2) notes:

> One of the more intriguing items is that in the lawsuit depositions, when the pilot Juan Rabero, a citizen of Puerto Real, says that he knows of the antiquity of the city because he has read it many times in the *Cronica* . . . this was probably the work of Oviedo y Valdes, *Historia General Y Natural de las Indias*, and indicates that there were some literate people, and doubtless books, in the town.

Excavations at Locus 19 confirm this supposition with the recovery of what appear to be several ornate brass and enamel book clasps (figure 6.15). The large clasps may have served some other purpose because they appear larger than those usually found on books of the period (cf. Penney 1967). Willis (1984:187–92) also found these items at Building A.

Bells. Called "hawk bells," these large (4 cm in diameter), copper-alloy, two-piece, spherical bells were a popular item in the early Indian trade. Willis (1984: figure 59a) suggests that they were used as horse ornaments. Ian Brown (1977, 1979) and Mitchem and McEwan (1988) discuss two types of hawk bells, "Clarksdale" and "flushloop," which, though similar in appearance, are different in manufacture and chronological range. The bells from Puerto Real are of the Clarksdale type, which is in keeping with Mitchem and McEwan's (1988:47) sixteenth-century chronological assignment.

Pipes. Three kaolin pipestems were recovered from late proveniences at Locus 19 and may represent a later disturbance by the French because the Spanish are known not to have used kaolin pipes extensively until the eighteenth century (Deagan 1983:246).

Other Personal Objects. Two keys and a blade from a pocket type of knife were discovered near the structure at Locus 19. Also included in this category were fragments of lead seals. These probably represent seals on bales of goods rather than individual personal seals. It is unfortunate that any stamps or marks on these seals had been obscured prior to recovery.

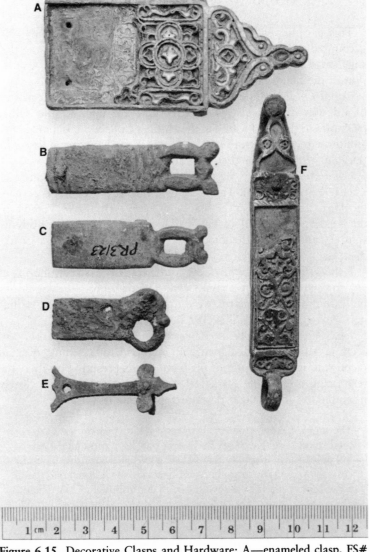

Figure 6.15. Decorative Clasps and Hardware: A—enameled clasp, FS# 3127; B—brass clasp, FS# 3165; C—brass clasp, FS# 3123; brass and iron buckle, FS# 3108; E—brass furniture escutcheon, FS# 3132; F— enameled clasp, FS# 3157 *(photo by James Quine; Florida Museum of Natural History Collection)*

Group 10 - Activity-Related Items

This became, essentially, a catchall category in this study that accounted for items inappropriate to other categories. As the title suggests, these items are associated with various activities. A selection of the identifiable items are discussed below.

Candleholder. Made of a copper alloy, this simple item consisted of a double-disk base stabilizing the tube holding a candle. Other examples of this are located in the Hodges Collection, Limbe, Haiti, and those recovered from La Vega Vieja in the Dominican Republic (Deagan 1987: personal communication).

Candlesnuffer. Two of these unusual artifacts were found at Locus 19 (figure 6.16). They resemble scissors, with small perpendicular plates resting on the blades themselves. In this way, the candle is extinguished and its wick trimmed at the same time. Both the snuffers and the candleholder were found in Late Period proveniences.

Fishing Items. These artifacts consisted of six iron fishhooks of varying sizes (between 2 and 3 cm). The discovery of these hooks indicate that the Spaniards were using lines to take fish as well as nets as suggested by Willis (1984:193).

Jew's Harps/Guimbardes. These artifacts are typically iron, 4 to 5 cm in length, and U-shaped with a constricted opening. A small metal stub is in the center of the basal curve, presumably where the resonating middle piece was attached (figure 6.17). They closely resemble the Jew's harps described by Crane (1972:20).

> The form of the instruments is in no way different from that of the modern ones; the Jew's harp may be the only instrument manufactured in Europe today in a form that has been unchanged for two-thousand years. . . . The early instruments are generally small, commonly about 5.0 x 2.5 cm or a little less in maximum dimensions. . . . The tongues, always of steel, have normally disintegrated, except for traces of rust at the point where they joined the frame.

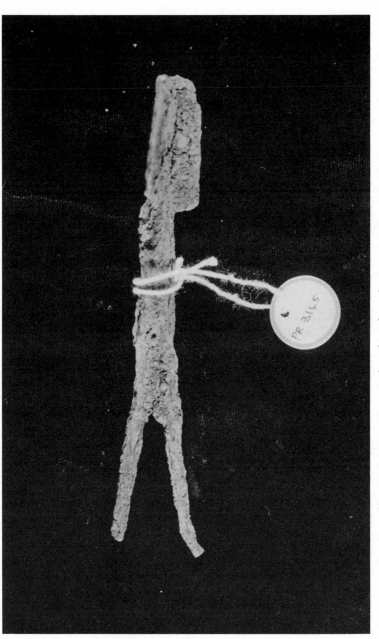

Figure 6.16. Candlesnuffer (FS# 3165, 13 cm in length) *(photo by James Quine; Florida Museum of Natural History Collection)*

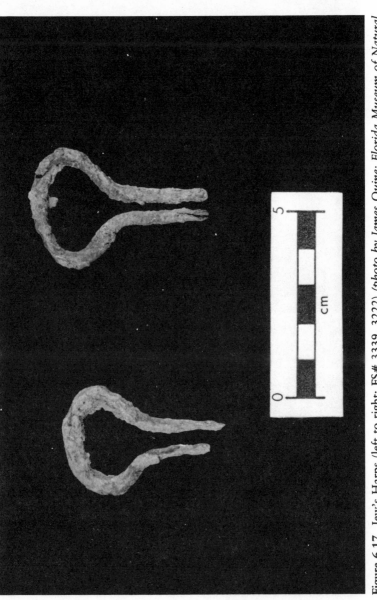

Figure 6.17. Jew's Harps (left to right: FS# 3339, 3222) (photo by James Quine; Florida Museum of Natural History Collection)

Group 13 - Furniture Hardware

A small category in numbers and types of artifacts, this one is composed primarily of brass tacks at Puerto Real (figure 6-10A). These would have served both a useful and decorative function when used to attach upholstery to furniture (cf. Eberlein 1925). Included in this category are two decorative escutcheons (see figure 6.15) and a drawer-pull. Interesting artifacts that may belong in this category are the flat, brass, perforated, star-shaped objects (figure 6.18). These have been variously interpreted as spur rowels or clothing ornaments and saddle ornaments (Radisch 1986). Radisch also suggests furniture decoration as a possibility. This seems to be more than just a possibility. The single hole in the center is suggestive of fastening by a single nail. Also, comparisons with known furniture hardware (Eberlein 1925:131–36) show striking similarities. The paucity of artifacts in this category can be explained by the Spanish tendency toward limited furniture use. What little furniture there was tended to be highly decorated (Eberlein 1925:viii).

Group 14 - Tools

Several different types of woodworking tools were found at Locus 19. Three chisels were present as well as a wedge and a fragment of a file. Iron punches and awls, identical to modern forms, were possibly used for leatherworking at the site. An iron plumb bob was recovered at Locus 19 from an Early Period context. One is tempted to speculate that it may have been used to assist in the layout and construction of the Late Period structure at the site. In any case, it is solid iron and egg-shaped with a flattened base and a knob on top to which a line could be attached. It is six cm in length.

Group 15 - Toys and Games

This is a difficult category in that many of its manifestations are not recognized as such in the archaeological record. Several

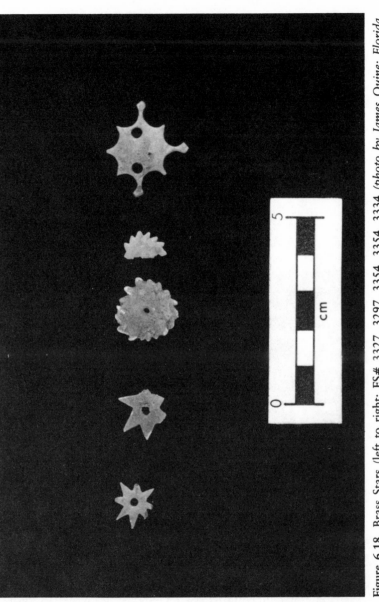

Figure 6.18. Brass Stars (left to right: FS# 3327, 3297, 3354, 3354, 3334 *(photo by James Quine; Florida Museum of Natural History Collection)*

"gaming disks" are reported from Locus 19. These were fashioned from various types of ceramics (olive jar, Columbia Plain, Christophe Plain) and were presumably used in some type of game, though James (1985) suggests their use as stoppers for olive jars. The whizzer, or whirligig, is a ceramic disk with two holes in the middle. It is operated by running a loop of string through the holes, twisting the string then pulling it tight causing the disk to spin. Noel-Hume (1978:321) states that "the majority were made from uninformative bits of scrap metal . . . copper coins or datable fragments of filed pottery."

Group 16 - Harness and Tack

Undoubtedly many pieces that served as horse tack are not listed in this category simply because they have not been recognized as such. A horseshoe fragment recovered from the midden outside the structure is unmistakably in this category. Less certain are several iron rings and rods similar to what Willis (1984: figure 55) referred to as horse tackle. Many small rectangular brass buckles were found. They measure 1.2 by 3.1 cm with one of the long sides decorated with a spiral twist. They are thought to have been associated with harness trappings, but no documentation has been found to this effect.

Group 17 - Religious Items

No religious items were found at Locus 19.

Group 18 - Miscellaneous Substances

Most of the artifacts in this category are raw materials and will not be discussed in depth with three exceptions. Several amethyst crystals were found in archaeological contexts at Locus 19. Locally available, their function to the inhabitants, if any, is not known, though they were valued as gems in Europe (Muller 1972). A coprolite from a small animal, possibly a dog, was recovered. The exact species of the animal responsible for this ecofact awaits further investigation from a competent scatologist. Finally, a small cake of blue, powdery substance resembling indigo dye was found in the midden desposits. This, too, awaits investigation.

Faunal Assemblage

A relatively wide variety of species are represented at Locus 19. These are listed by class in table 6.2. The fauna were quantified in taxonomic order (see appendix 2), but for interpretive purposes they can be divided into two groups; native and introduced species. These categories correspond to, with a couple of exceptions, wild versus domestic species. The introduced species include: dogs, cats, swine, cattle, sheep/goats, and chickens. The turtles, fish, and shellfish are all native species. All the large and medium mammal bones probably represent introduced species because no mammals of that size were native to Hispaniola. The large mammals probably correspond with cattle but without positive identification; zooarchaeological procedures require that such specimens be described rather than be assigned a speculative identification. The specimens of the family Anatidae (swans, geese, and ducks) are of uncertain affiliation. In these cases, the species in question could have been introduced ducks or migratory waterfowl.

The Cricetids, however, are an interesting anomaly. One specimen has been positively identified as *Neofiber alleni* (round-tailed muskrat), which is native to south Florida and has not been previously reported from Hispaniola (Charles Woods: personal communication). Its presence in an early context at Puerto Real could be explained by intra-Caribbean trade patterns. It was during the first half of the sixteenth century that the Bahamas were being depopulated by slave raids (Sauer 1966:159). It seems likely, by its very proximity, that the southern coast of Florida was also a target of these slavers. Perhaps the muskrat was taken (possibly for its pelt) during such a raid and transported to Puerto Real, which was one of the main ports servicing the slave trade. Whatever its route, the presence of this muskrat at Puerto Real demonstrates early contact between Hispaniola and Florida.

The minimum numbers of individuals for each species was calculated on the basis of the most numerous unique element of the species from a particular provenience. Such factors as age and size of the specimen were also taken into account. The biomass was determined using an allometric scaling technique based on skeletal mass. Underlying this technique is the premise that, by using a straight-line regression formula (Reitz 1974), skeletal weight can be correlated with body weight. The formula is:

Log Y = B (Log X) + Log A
Where: Y = Body weight in kg
         X = Skeletal weight in kg
         A = Y – Intercept
         B = Slope

The class values for Log A and B have been determined for each taxa by researchers at the Florida State Museum. To simplify matters further, Stephen Hale and Irvy Quitmeyer, of the Florida State Museum, have written a program for the Apple II series personal computer that performs the necessary calculations. Invertebrates are not yet included in those calculations.

The results of the biomass calculations are of interest. The five most important animals, in terms of biomass, at the site in descending order of importance were: Early Period—cattle, large mammals, swine, UID mammals, and pond turtles; Late Period—large mammals, UID mammals, cattle, swine, and pond turtles. It is interesting to compare these figures to the minimum number of individuals. Because biomass is used only on identifiable species, some change in order of importance is to be expected. However, there is quite a difference in the order of animals in both periods. Invertebrates were excluded from consideration because they were not included in the biomass comparisons. Based on the minimum number of individuals rather than biomass calculations, the animals were in the following order of importance: Early Period—pond turtles, swine, cattle, chickens, and bigmouth sleeper (fish). Late Period—pond turtles, swine, chickens, cattle, and mullet.

Table 6.2 Species Present at Puerto Real

Scientific Name	Common Name
MAMMALS	
Cricetidae	Rodent
Canis familiaris	Dog
Felis domesticus	Cat
Sus scrofa	Pig
Bos taurus	Cow
Neofiber alleni	Round-tail muskrat
Caprinae	Goat/sheep
BIRDS	
Anatidae	Swans, geese, ducks
Gallus gallus	Chicken
REPTILES	
Testudines	Turtles
Pseudemys sp.	Pond turtle
Chelonidae	Sea turtle
FISH	
Osteichthyes	Bony fishes
Megalops atlanticus	Tarpon
Elops saurus	Ladyfish
Albula vulpes	Bonefish
Centropomus undecimalis	Snook
Epinephelus sp.	Grouper
Mycteroperca sp.	Grouper
Caranx hippos	Crevalle jack
Lutjanus sp.	Snapper
Gerreidae	Mojarras
Haemulon sp.	Grunts

(Table 6.2 continued)

Scientific Name	Common Name
Sparidae	Porgy
Sciaenidae	Drum
Pomacathidae	Angelfish
Mugil sp.	Mullet
Gobiomorus dormitor	Bigmouth sleeper
INVERTEBRATES	
Decapoda	Crab
Brachyura	True crab
Cardisoma sp.	Land crab
Cittarium pica	W. I. top-shell
Nertina virginea	Virgin nerite
Strombus gigas	Queen conch
Arcidae	Ark
Brachidontes exustus	Scorched mussel
Mytilopsis cf. *leucopheta*	False mussel
Isognomon atlatus	Flat tree oyster
Crassostrea virginica	Easter oyster
Codakia costata	Costate lucine
Codakia orbicularis	Tiger lucine
Lucine pectinata	Thick lucina
Chama sp.	Jewel box
Tellina fausta	Faust tellin
Donax denticulata	Donax
Anomalocardia denticulata	W. I. pointed venus
Chione cancellata	Cross-barred venus

7

Results of Analyses

Excavations at Puerto Real have yielded a tremendous amount and variety of sixteenth-century Spanish artifacts. Yet, merely describing them falls short of their interpretive potential. The raw data presented in the preceding chapter can be interpreted in terms of the test implications proposed in chapter 4. The satisfaction of these test implications allows the proposal of a hypothesis concerning a general Spanish pattern of adaptation to the New World. This hypothesis, to reiterate, predicts that the material assemblage will reflect conservatism in those socially visible areas associated with male activities coupled with Spanish-Indian acculturation in the less visible female-dominated areas. The best way to test this hypothesis is to compare the material assemblage with what would be expected if the hypothesis were true.

Test 1

Food-preparation activities, as represented in the archaeological assemblage, should show a significant admixture of European and locally manufactured wares. In the initial stage of colonization, it would be expected that the locally available Taino Indian wares would have been used by the earliest settlers. It is furthermore expected that the nature of the locally manufactured items would have shifted from Indian- to African-influenced types through time.

An examination of the data reveals that 62 percent of the utilitarian wares (both Early and Late Periods combined) were of local origin, and the remaining 38 percent were composed of olive jar, green bacin, and other Hispanic wares. This clearly demonstrates a significant overall admixture of the two types of wares. Furthermore, this ratio held through time. In the Early Period, 64 percent of the utilitarian ceramics were locally made. This agreed closely with the 62 percent of the same ware category in the Late Period.

A close study of the group 4 (Colono and aboriginal) ceramics indicates a shift in the nature of the locally manufactured ceramics through time. The recognized Indian ceramic traditions, Meillac and Carrier, are never very common at Locus 19, accounting for less than 1 percent of the group 4 assemblage. Easily the most numerous type is Unidentified Plain pottery, which comprises 51 percent of the Early Period assemblage and 50 percent of the Late Period assemblage. Christophe Plain is the next most numerous, accounting for 37 percent and 40 percent of the Early and Late Period group 4 assemblages respectively.

Greg Smith (1986) found the same sort of distribution in his analysis of three loci at Puerto Real. He interpreted this as a replacement of aboriginal wares through time with African-made ceramics. The shifts in ceramic types mirror the demographic changes occurring in the labor force at Puerto Real. As the Indian population declined, it was replaced by imported African slaves. Smith claims that the distribution of Group 4 ceramics

> offers strong support for the replacement of Indian tradition ceramics through time, a replacement which was primarily accomplished through African ceramic manufacture. The cultural and temporal affiliation of Unidentified Plain pottery is not clearly apparent. Results seem to suggest that, while a response to the ceramic needs of the entire Puerto Real community, Unidentified Plain pottery may be the product of both Indian and African manufacture during the period of population upheaval. (1986:101)

Given the ceramic evidence, the first test implication supports the hypothesis.

Test 2

Status-related artifacts should be almost exclusively European in trade or manufacture. It would be expected that the attempts by New World settlers to maintain an Iberian life-style would be reflected in the use of articles from the Spanish empire in socially visible areas of daily life. Socially visible is the key term here because articles not normally seen by those outside the household (e.g., cookware) could hardly be expected to reflect the owner's status to others.

Status, as it is used in this work, refers to the individual's access to scarce resources that were desirable, but not easily obtainable. The higher the person's status, the greater the access to these desired, socially visible products. The determination of status in Spain was not entirely economic; hereditary factors *(limpieza de sangre)* were also involved. A workable definition of the Spanish hierarchical system would be the *estate* system of social stratification, which is

> a hierarchic society the strata of which are rigidly separated by law and customs and often characterized by different hereditary relationship to land (as owners, tenants, or serfs). Though social status is generally hereditary, vertical social mobility is not altogether excluded. . . . Under the estate system, the individual's status or prestige was of paramount importance notwithstanding the permanence of economic differences. (Morner 1967:7–8)

As mentioned in chapter 2, there came to be a close correlation between wealthy, *converso* merchants and prestigious, old Christian *hidalgos*. Through carefully arranged marriages, the *converso* families were able to legitimize their status, and the *hidalgos* achieved the financial status befitting their station. So, although economic and social status were not exactly equated in sixteenth-century Spain, a close enough relation occurred to warrant the use of hard-to-obtain Hispanic items in the archaeological record to identify persons of high status. In the colonies, one's relative status was closely related with how well one could maintain the Spanish life-style.

There are a number of socially visible areas where, according to the hypothesis, we would expect to find Hispanic artifacts. The table of the Spanish colonist would be one such place. Following the hypothesis, we would expect to find tablewares composed primarily of majolicas or other Hispanic wares. This is, indeed, exactly the case. There are *no* locally made ceramics in tableware forms (e.g., *platos, escudillas,* and *tazas*). Such copy wares have been found in Spanish colonial contexts such as San Luis (Vernon 1988). Additionally, many other high-status marker artifacts were recovered. Expensive articles from Spain's imperial trade network, such as Italian *latticinio*-decorated glass and Cologne stoneware from Germany, are not uncommon at Locus 19. These items were found in much smaller quantities at other locations in Puerto Real, strengthening the presumption of the high-status affiliation of Locus 19.

Evidence also indicates that a Spanish woman was a resident at Locus 19. This is suggested by the presence of the beads, a unicorn pendant, and a jet ring. The additional evidence of lace tatting as an activity at the site (the lace bobbin described in chapter 6) indicates that this woman was Hispanic rather than native. Although no list of women was found during the literature search (Lyon 1981), some Spanish women were certainly present at Puerto Real. The *repartimiento* of 1514 does indicate that, of the twenty *vecinos* at Puerto Real, three had Castilian wives (Sauer 1966:199).

Emigration of women to the New World was not uncommon, but tended to focus on established large towns. Prior to the discovery of New Spain, Santo Domingo was the chief destination of Spanish women; after discovery and settlement, Peru and Mexico were the favored destinations (Boyd-Bowman 1976:596–99). Because a Spanish woman at a colonial outpost town such as Puerto Real would have been comparatively rare, her presence at Locus 19 would be expected at a high-status household capable of supporting such a personage. It is also possible that children would have been at the site. The toy "whizzer" recovered there may have belonged to the resident's child.

In the area of clothing, there is, as expected, strong retention of European styles. More than 160 aglets (lacing tips) were found as well as a variety of buckles and buttons of various composition.

The native style of dress was to "go naked as they were born, except that over their privates they wear a loincloth, of linen or some other kind of cloth" (Oviedo 1959:13). The clothing accessories mentioned above would not have been necessary had the colonists adopted the Indian's fashions. It may seem obvious that the Spanish colonists would not have "gone native" so far as clothing was concerned. However, the existence of the array of fasteners gives positive material verification to the implicit assumptions that have been based on documentary records. It also reenforces the interpretation of the occupant's status. The clothing of the lower classes was extremely simple (Braudel 1985:316), having a minimum of metal accessories. Also found at Locus 19 was a silver aglet, further strengthening the argument for a high-status resident.

Little jewelry or religious paraphernalia have been recovered at Puerto Real. Rather than an indication of low status or religious indifference, this probably reflects the manner in which such objects enter the archaeological record. Small, valuable items such as these usually are deposited as the result of loss rather than discard (Schiffer 1972). Very little of the interior of the structure was actually excavated, where such losses would be most likely to occur, or at least be recovered. The value of these items would also mitigate against the loss of a great many of them in that greater care would be taken of such possessions. Beads were a popular trade item. Perhaps their presence outside the structure can be accounted for by the traffic in that area of the non-Hispanic inhabitants. The excavation of several pieces of book hardware suggest the presence of literate people at Locus 19. Because books were something of a rarity in the sixteenth century as well as the ability to read them (Braudel 1985:40), this might be another indication of a high-status household.

Test 3

Structures at Puerto Real should employ local materials in their construction; however, the architectural style of the buildings and physical layout of the town should be Hispanic in nature. This implication follows from the hypothesized Spanish affiliations in highly visible areas of colonial culture, and also from mandated urban-planning designs from the Crown (Zendegui 1977).

Although the site had been extensively robbed of its building materials by post-sixteenth-century occupants and archaeological excavation has not been extensive, enough data were collected to satisfy the tests of the third implication. The building materials appear to have been obtained locally. The stone came from the mountains just inland from the site. Outcrops of this type of rock are visible in that area today. Given the limited cargo space aboard the infrequent vessels calling at Puerto Real, it would seem logical that the masonry might have also been manufactured locally. However, Willis (1984:84) recovered a brick with a script pattern etched on one of its surfaces. He suggests that this was a lot-shipment mark indicating that the brick was made in Spain for shipment to the Indies. Compositional analysis would have to be performed to determine positively the place of origin of the bricks and barrel tile.

The fact that stone and masonry building materials were found argues against an aboriginal architectural style. As discussed in chapter 4, the Taino *bohio* was constructed of cane, mud, and straw. The layout of the structure (see figure 5.5) also is not in keeping with the circular floor plan typical of the indigenous structures. The linear wall foundation probably represents the facade of a residential structure with an attached walled courtyard or the back wall of an enclosed courtyard, both of which are representative of Spanish architecture (Manucy 1978).

The structure, itself, may have utilized the western portion of the wall. Three pieces of evidence lead to this conclusion. The drains are located at this end and would have serviced the house, emptying to the north. The brick-paved area is on the interior (southern) side of the western section of the wall. It may have served as flooring for part of the structure (Eberlein 1925:v). The midden was located just north of the western portion of the wall. The association between a house and an area of refuse is explained by the documentary record. A sixteenth-century ordinance for the city of Madrid forbade the disposal of "water, refuse, or other things" from windows and balconies. These were to be disposed of through the front door at prescribed times to avoid hitting passersby (Defourneaux 1979:63).

Such an ordinance may not have been specifically in effect at Puerto Real, but the behavioral pattern may have followed from Spain. The alternative is that the foundation was the base of the back wall of an enclosed courtyard. The midden represents trash disposal behind this back wall. Unfortunately, much of the area south of the wall had been disturbed by the construction of a large drainage canal by French planters, thus obscuring any interior details of the structure.

The excavations at Puerto Real have provided an opportunity to determine whether the official town plan decreed in the latter half of the sixteenth century was put into effect to correct haphazard town planning or whether it was merely a formalization of an urban design already in effect.

The archaeological excavation grid established by Willis, upon which all subsequent work has followed, was initially set in at an angle 30 degrees east of magnetic north so as to coincide with the alignment of Building A (Willis 1984:50–57). The fence line delineated in the 1981 field season (McEwan 1983) and the wall foundation uncovered during the 1984–85 field season were both perfectly aligned with this grid.

Classic grid-pattern towns are built around a central plaza, upon which face important buildings, such as the church, and which often served as a marketplace. Willis's (1984) excavations in the center of the site uncovered a structure that he identified as a church, adjacent to which was a market area. Building B, excavated by Marrinan (1982) and also located at the center of the site, appears to be another large public building. The masonry concentrations delineated by Williams (1986) form a fairly regular pattern around the central area of the site (see figure 5.1). Thus, it appears that, at least at Puerto Real, the grid town plan needed no royal edict to enforce its use.

Test 4

The diet of the colonist should show a mixture of the Iberian barnyard complex of peninsular Spain and the mixed hunting-fishing strategies of the indigenous peoples. Specifically, this would entail the abandonment of traditional resources unsuited to the new environment; the incorporation of aboriginal patterns of wild faunal exploitation; and development of a domestic-animal industry utilizing those species suited to the new environment.

When the Spaniards arrived in the Caribbean, virtually no large mammals were on Hispaniola (Parry and Sherlock 1971:2). The colonists did, however, bring a number of domesticated animals with them, including cattle, swine, sheep, horses, dogs, and cats (Oviedo 1959:11). Many of these animals did quite well in their new environment. So well, in fact, that Oviedo (1959:11) claimed that many had run wild, especially cattle, swine, cats, and dogs.

The reason many imported mammals prospered on Hispaniola is that they encountered virtually no competition because there were no native ruminants. The native fauna were primarily avian or aquatic rather than terrestrial. The terrestrial fauna that *did* exist were restricted to rodents, turtles, and other reptiles.

The overall pattern of the faunal assemblage recovered from Locus 19 is similar to that recovered from Loci 33 and 35 (Area 35) by McEwan (1983). This is not surprising because that area is also believed to be a high-status residence within the city.

The fauna from Loci 33/35 were overwhelmingly mammal. In terms of biomass, cattle was the most prevalent taxa in this category with swine a close second. Pond turtles (*Pseudemys* sp.) were a surprisingly large contributor to the colonists' diet, ranking just below swine. Their contribution appeared to increase through time. The combined avian and fish remains totaled less than 1 percent of the overall faunal assemblage (McEwan 1983:82–90).

Mammals also dominated the assemblage at Locus 19, accounting for 96 percent of the total biomass (see table 7.3). Here again, cattle were most prevalent, followed by swine. Pond turtles were the third most important identifiable species, but accounted for only 4 percent of the total biomass as opposed to 7 percent at Loci 33 and 35. Even so, one must concur with McEwan (1983:91) that pond turtles were the major dietary adaptation of the Spanish colonists. However, they were not the only native species being used.

The colonists at Puerto Real consumed a wide variety of fish and shellfish. Fish in the assemblage included tarpon, bonefish, mullet, jack, and snappers. All these species inhabit shallow coastal waters or a brackish estuarine environment. Artifacts (e.g., net weights and fish hooks) indicate that both nets and hooks were used to procure them.

It is difficult to determine who was doing the fishing. It would seem unlikely that a high-status Spaniard would stoop to the manual labor of food gathering. There is the possible exception of an occasional sport-fishing venture. The alternative is that slaves were responsible for supplying the household with its fish (as well as other foodstuffs, no doubt). This implies that Spanish fishing technologies were adopted.

Fish may have actually contributed more to the diet than is apparent from the faunal sample. Recovery methods employed one-quarter-inch mesh to screen the excavated soil; screen of this size mesh has been shown to be likely to miss many of the small and fragile fish bones (Casteel 1972). However, flotation of soil samples did not significantly increase the sample.

Another factor arguing for greater fish consumption than is represented in the faunal sample is Catholicism. The Catholic calendar called for 166 meatless days, including Lent (Braudel 1985:214). Given the documentary evidence, artifactual evidence, and recovery bias, it seems possible that fish occupied a more important place in the diet than the faunal record indicates, but how much more cannot be determined at this time. Turtles, being aquatic, may also have been considered nonmeat by the Spaniards. Thus, their presence in the faunal assemblage may be connected to the Catholic calendar.

Perhaps even more interesting than the intrasite comparison is an intersite comparison with the nearby aboriginal site at En Bas Saline. How did the Spanish colonial diet differ from that of the native inhabitants? The faunal assemblage at En Bas Saline could be divided into pre- and post-contact time periods. More than sixty different species were identified at En Bas Saline as opposed to forty-six at Puerto Real. An even stronger contrast is seen when comparing the different faunal categories by biomass totals (table 7.1). Fish, even given the same collection biases, is the most important category in the pre-contact faunal assemblage at En Bas Saline (the post-contact assemblage will not be discussed here because the question of Spanish impact on the native society is beyond the scope of this work). Next in abundance were mammals, but these were small rodents rather than the large domesticates of the Europeans. Reptiles make up 9 percent of the aboriginal fauna, but, unlike the Europeans who focused almost exclusively on pond turtles, the natives at En Bas Saline also exploited sea turtles, iguanas, and snakes. A flightless rail, recently extinct, was the only bird species identified in the assemblage. Finally, like the Spaniards at Puerto Real, the Indians used a wide variety of invertebrate species. Because the biomass estimates for invertebrates were not comparable with those used for the vertebrates, their importance in the aboriginal diet cannot be assessed at this time.

The patterns of faunal exploitation appear very different between the two cultures. Clearly, the major factor involved is the introduction and success of domestic animals at the site. At St. Augustine, this was also apparent, though wild terrestrial animals formed a relatively more important part of the high-status individual's diet (Reitz and Cumbaa 1983). This difference from Puerto Real makes sense when one realizes the chief wild animal available in St. Augustine was white-tailed deer as opposed to the spiny rat, or hutia, of Hispaniola. McEwan (1983:98) concludes that "the difference in subsistence adaptation recognized archaeologically among Spanish New World colonies is thought to reflect the environmental parameters and the diverse composition and motives of the Spaniards in the respective settlements."

Table 7.1 Biomass: Puerto Real versus En Bas Saline

| Taxa | Early | | Late | | EBS | |
	Wgt. (kg)	%	Wgt.	%	Wgt.	%
Mammal	218.5	96	211.7	95	2.06	20
Avian	1.5	1>	.7	1>	.29	3
Reptile	6.7	3	8.7	4	.92	9
Fish	1.7	1>	1.2	1>	6.79	68

On the basis of the Puerto Real faunal data, it is concluded that the environmental parameters for wild-species availability and the success of Old World domesticates is the most important factor in determining the diet of the colonists.

Test 5

According to this test, the artifact and faunal assemblage would reflect a crystallization of the proposed Hispanic-American colonial pattern through time. It was stated in chapter 4 that this should be apparent in all the above test implications when viewed through time. Specifically, variations among households from this predicted pattern should become less evident in later periods. In light of the limited time of occupation, determining this could present a problem.

A major handicap is the division of occupation into only two periods. Do changes between the Early and Late Periods reflect a final, crystallized adaptive pattern or is this only a stage in an ongoing process of adaptation? That is, does the Late Period represent a plateau in a graph of culture change or is it only a point along a linear regression? Fortunately, the pattern is such at Puerto Real that the question of adaptive shift through time is quickly answered.

At Puerto Real, the matter of adaptive response was resolved early in the occupation. The Spanish colonists quickly adopted the "Spanish colonial pattern" tested in this work and retained it. This is demonstrable in both the artifact and faunal assemblages. As can be seen from table 7.2, the total quantity of artifacts differ through time, but little difference occurs through time in the proportional distribution of artifacts *within* specific functional and typological categories. For example, only 1,400 fragments of majolica were in the Early Period artifact assemblage as opposed to 4,574 pieces in the Late Period assemblage. However, in relation to the total number of artifacts in the respective assemblages, majolica made up 18.15 percent of the Early Period assemblage and 19.12 percent of the Late Period assemblage, a proportional difference of less than 1 percent. This similarity can be noted in virtually every artifact category.

Table 7.2 Early vs Late Contexts at Puerto Real

Category		Early	Late
Majolica	#	1,400	7,682
	%	18.15	19.12
Hispanic Tablewares	#	139	1,513
	%	1.80	3.75
European Utilitarian Wares	#	1,963	10,870
	%	25.45	26.93
European Tablewares	#	36	163
	%	.47	.40
Colono and Aboriginal Wares	#	3,526	17,387
	%	45.72	43.07
Kitchen Artifacts	#	232	1,037
	%	3.01	2.57
Structural Hardware	#	226	1,107
	%	2.93	2.74
Weaponry and Armor	#	8	15
	%	.10	.04
Clothing and Sewing Items	#	116	297
	%	1.50	.74
Personal Items and Jewelry	#	24	169
	%	.31	.42
Activity-Related Items	#	24	38
	%	.31	.09
Furniture Hardware	#	1	9
	%	.03	.04
Tools	#	2	18
	%	.03	.02
Toys and Games	#	2	9
	%	.03	.02
Harness and Tack	#	12	19
	%	.16	.05

Some shifts in particular artifact types can be noted, but this has to do with replacement of styles and fashion *within* functional categories. That is, within a functional category (e.g., majolica), certain types of majolica might decline in popularity through time and be replaced by new types. This does not affect the category's ranking in respect to the other categories. The value of this waxing and waning of types through time for the archaeologist is as a chronological tool. The primary dating tool of the historical archaeologist is the *terminus post quem* of various "marker" ceramic types. This tool, together with stratigraphic positioning, was used to differentiate the Early from the Late Period at Locus 19.

Table 7.3 Biomass Comparisons at Puerto Real

Taxa	L. 19 Early		L. 19 Late		L. 33/35	
	Wgt. (kg)	%	Wgt.	%	Wgt.	%
Mammal	218.513	96	211.693	95	310.658	92
Avian	1.46	<1	.74	<1	.475	<1
Reptile	6.73	3	8.72	4	24.895	7
Fish	1.667	<1	1.197	<1	1.085	<1

The consistency in faunal patterning is even more apparent. Table 7.3 depicts an almost unchanged faunal assemblage through time at Locus 19. The faunal assemblage from Loci 33 and 35 could not be put in either a late or an early category, and should be considered simply as being from the sixteenth century (McEwan 1983:147). The faunal pattern from Loci 33 and 35 also conforms closely to the faunal pattern delineated at Locus 19. Again, this suggests a continuity through time rather than a slowly crystallizing adaptive shift.

8

Summary and Conclusions

Summary

Excavations at Locus 19 have shown it to be a high-status residence occupied primarily during the latter half of the sixteenth century. These conclusions are based on the amount and type of refuse associated with the structure and the relatively high proportion of Hispanic to aboriginal ceramics. There is evidence of an early sixteenth-century occupation at the site, though its exact nature could not be determined. The Late Period structure was located 100 m north of the town plaza and is interpreted as a residence with an attached walled courtyard.

Living in this large residence was a relatively wealthy Spaniard, his Spanish wife, and possibly a child. The interior of their home and possessions reflected the high status of the family. Their table was set with fine majolicas and Italian glassware. Their clothing followed the fashions prevalent in Spain. In another area of the house, slaves, probably African, prepared the food they had collected in cooking vessels they had made. Their master, judging by the abundance of coins and leather-working tools, may have been a merchant dealing in hides and slaves. The porcelain in his household suggests that at least some of his business was conducted illicitly with the Portuguese corsairs who frequented the harbor.

The interpretation of the layout and function of Locus 19 serves

115

as a backdrop to the true goal of the project: identifying patterns in the material culture that reflect the changes that the Spaniards underwent on their way to becoming creoles. In St. Augustine, Deagan (1983) determined that male-oriented, socio-technic artifacts were Hispanic in nature; and female-oriented, technomic artifacts showed evidence of acculturation with the non-Hispanic population. The present study was concerned with how Spaniards, in general, changed as a result of their colonial experiences. The accomplishment of this goal involved testing the applicability of the patterning of the material culture at one Spanish colonial site to a different Spanish colonial site in order to determine pan-Hispanic regularities in the archaeological record.

Conclusions based on the results of the analyses tend to support the hypothesized pattern of Spanish colonial adaptation. Ceramics associated with low social visibility food preparation and storage activities *do* show a significant admixture of European and locally manufactured ceramics. Tablewares, ornamentation, clothing items, and other highly visible status items *were* almost exclusively European in origin. The structure, as far as can be determined, *was* built in accordance with Spanish architectural traditions and new ideas concerning urban planning. This pattern appears to have changed little through time. The alternative would have been an incorporation of non-Hispanic traits into the socio-technic as well as the technomic sphere of artifacts, but this did not occur.

The material patterning at Puerto Real closely resembles that of St. Augustine in terms of the ceramic-assemblage categories. Specific items in the other categories reflect the different activities of the site's inhabitants. A significant general difference from St. Augustine can be seen in the faunal pattern. As discussed in the previous chapter, this is probably due to the differing environmental constraints placed upon the preferred Iberian foodways. The colonial diet was clearly different than aboriginal subsistence practices. The primary variable in the differences among the diets of the Indians, the Spanish colonists at St. Augustine, and the Spanish colonists at Puerto Real appears to have been the success of the domesticates that were introduced. The primary difference from peninsular Spain was the relative abundance of meat, specifically beef and pork.

Conclusions

What can be concluded from the research at Puerto Real? This was one of the first European settlements in the part of the world that has come to be known as Latin America. Foster (1960:2) states: "Hispanic America can be thought of as an enormous culture area, modern in origin, distinct from British America and from all other world areas." Even early Latin America was recognized as socially if not culturally distinct from Spain. Offspring of the colonists, born in the New World, were called creoles and treated differently from those born in peninsular Spain (cf. Morner 1967, McAlister 1963).

This early Hispanic-American culture was an unequal amalgam of Spanish and Native American cultural traits. Research at Puerto Real allows the delineation of those areas that were primarily Spanish and those that received non-Hispanic influences. It appears that outwardly the cultural pattern was composed primarily of Hispanic traits (e.g., dress, architecture, and interior furnishings). Non-Hispanic traits, at least as seen in the material assemblage, are found in areas traditionally associated with women's activities, specifically food-preparation technologies. The conclusion gained through archaeological research confirms the Hispanic-American cultural pattern suggested by Deagan (1974) for St. Augustine. Specifically it is a synthesis of male Spanish traits and female non-Hispanic traits. That the Spanish traits appear most visible is a reflection of social conditions during the sixteenth century.

In summary, this study tested the pan-Hispanicity of the colonial pattern developed at St. Augustine. Identification of a pan-Hispanic response to colonialism is a step toward the development of a general pattern of colonial adaptation.

To reiterate, the hypothesis was supported by the evidence recovered at Puerto Real. The pattern does seem to have applicability beyond St. Augustine. This does not exclude the possibility that other explanations exist for the data, but it does allow continued use of the hypothesis to guide future research. Truth is, after all, only the best current hypothesis. With this in mind, new hypotheses can be generated to test on new data awaiting excavation at Puerto Real.

On a more general, anthropological scale, the model of colonial adaptation developed for Hispanic sites can be tested at non-Hispanic colonial sites in the Americas. Did the French and British adapt to their new surroundings in a manner similar to the Spanish? If not, how did they differ and what factors might account for these differences? Again, the model tested at Puerto Real can serve as a null hypothesis for these inquiries.

Appendix 1

Artifacts Recovered from Locus 19

MAJOLICAS

Artifact	Period		Total
	Early	Late	
Bisque			
#	39	221	260
%	2.79	2.86	2.85
Caparra Blue			
#	8	7	15
%	.57	.09	.16
Columbia Plain			
#	1,183	6,490	7,673
%	84.50	84.09	84.15
Columbia Plain Green			
#	33	153	186
%	2.36	1.98	2.04
Cuenca Tile			
#	1	0	1
%	.07	0	.01
Isabella Polychrome			
#	1	11	12
%	.07	.14	.13

MAJOLICAS (CONTINUED)

Artifact	Period		
	Early	Late	Total
La Vega Blue on White			
#	0	3	3
%	0	.04	.03
Ligurian Blue on Blue			
#	0	11	11
%	0	.14	.12
Lusterware			
#	0	1	1
%	0	.01	.01
Montelupo Polychrome			
#	0	9	9
%	0	.12	.10
Puerto Real Green and Green			
#	4	20	24
%	.29	.26	.26
Santa Elena Green and White			
#	9	36	45
%	.64	.47	.49
Sevilla Blue on Blue			
#	0	3	3
%	0	.04	.03
Sevilla Blue on White			
#	0	1	1
%	0	.01	.01
Santo Domingo Blue on White			
#	1	15	16
%	.07	.19	.17
Yayal Blue on White			
#	4	66	70
%	.29	.86	.77
White Majolica			
#	42	295	337
%	3.00	3.82	3.70
Polychrome Majolica			
#	17	102	119
%	1.21	1.32	1.31

MAJOLICAS (CONTINUED)

Artifact	Period		Total
	Early	Late	
UID Blue on White			
#	58	274	332
%	4.14	3.55	3.64
Total	1,400	7,718	9,118

UTILITARIAN CERAMICS

Artifact	Period		Total
	Early	Late	
El Morro			
#	1	2	3
%	.05	.02	.03
Green bacin			
#	62	284	346
%	3.16	2.61	2.70
Lead-glazed coarse earthenware			
#	221	990	1,211
%	11.26	9.11	9.44
Olive jar			
#	733	5,583	6,316
%	37.34	51.36	49.22
Olive jar, glazed			
#	392	1,484	1,876
%	19.97	13.65	14.61
Redware			
#	51	269	320
%	2.60	2.40	2.50
Spanish storage jar			
#	24	3	27
%	1.22	.03	.21
Spanish storage jar, glazed			
#	1	22	23
%	.05	.20	.18

UTILITARIAN CERAMICS (CONTINUED)

Artifact	Period		
	Early	Late	Total
UID coarse earthenware			
#	478	2,233	2,711
%	24.35	20.54	21.12
Total	1,963	10,870	12,833

EUROPEAN TABLEWARES

Artifact	Period		
	Early	Late	Total
Cologne stoneware			
#	1	24	25
%	2.78	14.72	12.56
Delft			
#	1	4	5
%	2.78	2.45	2.51
Faience			
#	7	27	34
%	19.44	16.56	17.09
Lead-glazed coarse earthenware			
#	2	26	28
%	5.56	15.95	14.07
Ming porcelain			
#	0	45	45
%	0	27.61	22.61
UID tin-enameled ware			
#	25	37	62
%	69.44	22.70	31.15
Total	36	163	199

HISPANIC TABLEWARES

Artifact	Period		
	Early	Late	Total
Feldspar inlaid			
#	9	253	262
%	6.72	16.67	15.86
Melado			
#	125	459	584
%	93.28	30.24	35.35
Orange micaceous			
#	0	806	806
%	0	53.09	48.79
Total	134	1,518	1,652

COLONO AND ABORIGINAL CERAMICS

Artifact	Period		
	Early	Late	Total
UID decorated			
#	19	89	108
%	.48	.53	.51
UID plain			
#	1,811	8,648	10,459
%	51.33	49.74	50.00
Carrier			
#	3	10	13
%	.09	.06	.06
Christophe Plain			
#	1,319	6,897	8,216
%	37.39	39.65	39.27
Meillac			
#	46	99	145
%	1.30	.57	.69
Meillac-like			
#	9	6	15
%	.26	.03	.07

COLONO AND ABORIGINAL CERAMICS (CONTINUED)

Artifact	Period		Total
	Early	Late	
Red slipped			
#	319	1,638	1,957
%	9.04	9.42	9.36
Total	3,526	17,387	20,913

KITCHEN ARTIFACTS

Artifact	Period		Total
	Early	Late	
Decanter top			
#	0	3	3
%	0	.29	.24
Glass, aqua			
#	3	19	22
%	1.30	1.83	1.74
Glass, blue			
#	4	26	30
%	1.73	2.51	2.37
Glass, clear			
#	129	439	568
%	55.41	42.04	44.48
Glass, green			
#	50	184	234
%	21.65	17.74	18.45
Glass, *latticinio*-decorated			
#	38	316	354
%	16.45	30.47	27.92
Glass, polychrome			
#	1	1	2
%	.43	.10	.16
Glass, purple			
#	1	0	1
%	.43	0	.08

KITCHEN ARTIFACTS (CONTINUED)

Artifact	Period		Total
	Early	Late	
Glass, red			
#	0	1	1
%	0	.10	.08
Glass, UID			
#	1	5	6
%	.43	.48	.47
Glass, yellow			
#	0	1	1
%	0	.10	.08
Griddle			
#	2	29	31
%	.87	2.80	2.44
Handle			
#	2	0	2
%	.87	0	.16
Knife			
#	1	5	6
%	.43	.48	.47
Mano			
#	0	2	2
%	0	.19	.16
Metate			
#	0	1	1
%	0	.10	.08
Total	232	1,029	1,261

STRUCTURAL HARDWARE

Artifact	Period		Total
	Early	Late	
Bolt			
#	1	1	2
%	.44	.09	.14
UID pin			
#	5	15	20
%	2.18	1.35	1.50
Door lock			
#	0	2	2
%	0	.18	.15
Hinge			
#	0	3	2
%	0	.27	.22
Nail, wrought			
#	199	1,008	1,207
%	86.90	90.97	90.27
Spike, wrought			
#	19	56	75
%	8.30	5.05	5.61
Staple			
#	0	1	1
%	0	.09	.07
Tack, wrought			
#	2	18	20
%	.87	1.62	1.50
Washer			
#	0	3	3
%	0	.27	.22
Total	226	1,107	1,333

WEAPONRY AND ARMOR

Artifact	Period		
	Early	Late	Total
Lead shot			
#	0	1	1
%	0	9.09	7.69
Brigandine plate			
#	0	3	3
%	0	27.27	23.08
Chain mail			
#	0	5	5
%	0	45.45	38.46
Musket ball			
#	1	2	3
%	50.00	18.18	23.08
Spear			
#	1	0	2
%	50.00	0	7.69
Total	2	11	13

CLOTHING AND SEWING ITEMS

Artifact	Period		
	Early	Late	Total
Aglet			
#	38	125	163
%	32.76	42.09	39.47
Lace bobbin			
#	0	1	1
%	0	.34	.24
Buckle			
#	1	9	10
%	.86	3.03	2.42
Button, brass			
#	0	1	1
%	0	.34	.24

CLOTHING AND SEWING ITEMS (CONTINUED)

Artifact	Period		Total
	Early	Late	
Button, jet			
#	0	1	1
%	0	.34	.24
Button, pewter			
#	0	1	1
%	0	.34	.24
Button, silver			
#	0	3	3
%	0	1.01	.73
Clasp			
#	1	0	1
%	.86	0	.24
Fastener			
#	0	2	2
%	0	.67	.48
Hook and eye			
#	0	1	1
%	0	.34	.24
Scissors			
#	1	1	2
%	.86	.34	.48
Straight pin, brass			
#	75	148	223
%	64.66	49.83	54.00
Straight pin, iron			
#	0	1	1
%	0	.34	.24
Thimble			
#	0	3	3
%	0	1.01	.73
Total	116	297	413

PERSONAL ITEMS

Artifact	Period		
	Early	Late	Total
Bead, amber			
#	0	2	2
%	0	1.18	1.04
Bead, bone			
#	0	2	2
%	0	1.18	1.04
Bead, tubular chevron			
#	1	9	10
%	4.55	5.33	5.18
Bead, carnelian			
#	0	1	1
%	0	.59	.52
Bead, ceramic			
#	0	1	1
%	0	.59	.52
Bead, chevron			
#	1	7	8
%	4.55	4.14	4.15
Bead, crumb			
#	0	1	1
%	0	.59	.52
Bead, shell			
#	0	1	1
%	0	.59	.52
Bead, stone			
#	0	1	1
%	0	.59	.52
Bead, UID			
#	1	9	10
%	4.55	4.84	4.75
Hawk bell (Clarksdale bell)			
#	0	3	3
%	0	1.78	1.55
Book hardware			
#	3	2	5
%	13.64	1.18	2.59

PERSONAL ITEMS (CONTINUED)

Artifact	Period		
	Early	Late	Total
Maravedi			
#	15	120	135
%	68.18	71.01	69.95
Ring, jet			
#	1	0	1
%	4.55	0	.52
Key			
#	0	2	2
%	0	1.18	1.04
Knife, pocket			
#	0	1	1
%	0	.59	.52
Pendant			
#	0	1	1
%	0	.59	.52
Pipestem, kaolin			
#	0	3	3
%	0	1.79	1.57
Seal			
#	0	4	4
%	0	2.37	2.07
Total	22	168	191

ACTIVITY-RELATED ITEMS

Artifact	Period		
	Early	Late	Total
Candleholder			
#	0	1	1
%	0	3.12	2.08
Chain			
#	0	5	5
%	0	15.63	10.42

ACTIVITY-RELATED ITEMS (CONTINUED)

Artifact	Period		
	Early	Late	Total
Crucible			
#	1	1	2
%	6.25	3.12	4.17
Fishhook			
#	0	6	6
%	0	18.75	12.50
Grater			
#	9	6	15
%	56.25	18.75	31.25
Hook			
#	3	11	14
%	18.75	34.37	29.17
Hoop			
#	3	0	3
%	18.75	0	6.25
Snuffer			
#	0	2	2
%	0	6.25	4.17
Total	16	32	48

FURNITURE HARDWARE

Artifact	Period		
	Early	Late	Total
Tack, brass			
#	0	12	12
%	0	70.59	57.14
Escutcheon			
#	0	2	2
%	0	11.76	9.52
Furniture hardware			
#	4	3	7
%	100.00	17.64	33.33
Total	4	17	21

TOOLS

Artifact	Period		
	Early	Late	Total
Awl			
#	0	9	9
%	0	50.00	45.00
Chisel			
#	0	3	3
%	0	16.67	15.00
File			
#	0	1	1
%	0	5.56	5.00
Plumb bob			
#	1	0	1
%	50.00	0	5.00
Punch			
#	1	2	3
%	50.00	11.11	15,00
UID, tool			
#	0	2	2
%	0	11.11	10.00
Wedge			
#	0	1	1
%	0	5.56	5.00
Total	2	18	20

TOYS AND GAMES

Artifact	Period		
	Early	Late	Total
Gaming disk			
#	1	8	9
%	50.00	50.00	81.82
Marble			
#	0	1	1
%	0	11.11	9.09

TOYS AND GAMES (CONTINUED)

Artifact	Period		
	Early	Late	Total
Whizzer			
#	1	0	1
%	50.00	0	9.09
Total	2	9	11

HARNESS AND TACK

Artifact	Period		
	Early	Late	Total
Buckle			
#	1	8	9
%	8.33	42.11	29.03
Horse hardware			
#	3	2	5
%	25.00	10.53	16.13
Horseshoe			
#	1	0	1
%	8.33	0	3.20
Ring			
#	7	9	16
%	58.33	47.37	51.61
Total	12	19	31

Appendix 2

Fauna Recovered from Locus 19

MAMMALIAN FAUNA

Taxa Period	#	Wgt. (g)	MNI	Biomass (kg)
Arteriodactyla				
Early	—	—	—	—
Late	51	390.3	—	5.65
Bos taurus				
E	165	9,902.65	13	103.79
L	106	2,730.3	7	32.55
Canis familiaris				
E	—	—	—	—
L	6	2.6	1	.06
Caprinae				
E	9	10.4	1	.22
L	3	8.15	2	.17
Cricetidae				
E	2	0.1	1	.003
L	—	—	—	—
Felis sp.				
E	1	0.9	1	.02
L	2	0.9	1	.02

MAMMALIAN FAUNA (CONTINUED)

Taxa Period	#	Wgt. (g)	MNI	Biomass (kg)
UID mammal, large				
E	1,735	6,038.9	—	66.51
L	2,445	9,430.6	—	99.33
UID mammal, medium				
E	1	0.5	—	.01
L	15	8.0	—	.17
UID mammal				
E	2,420	1,200.2	—	15.54
L	9,214	4,233.15	—	48.31
Sus scrofa				
E	307	2,717.6	18	32.42
L	346	2,075.6	9	25.43

AVIAN FAUNA

Taxa Period	#	Wgt. (g)	MNI	Biomass (kg)
Anatidae				
E	1	.7	1	.01
L	—	—	—	—
Gallus gallus				
E	54	75.45	8	1.04
L	37	26.10	8	.40
Galliformes				
E	—	—	—	—
L	4	3.05	—	.06
Aves				
E	90	26.9	—	.41
L	62	17.5	—	.28

REPTILIAN FAUNA

Taxa Period	#	Wgt. (g)	MNI	Biomass (kg)
Chelonidae				
E	—	—	—	—
L	2	8.8	1	.14
Pseudemys sp.				
E	876	1,642.9	21	4.51
L	1,315	1,879.7	18	4.94
Testudines				
E	1,202	569.5	—	2.22
L	2,278	1,193.9	—	3.64

FISH

Taxa Period	#	Wgt. (g)	MNI	Biomass (kg)
Albula vulpes				
E	—	—	—	—
L	1	.5	1	.02
Carangidae				
E	2	1.5	—	.05
L	—	—	—	—
Caranx hippos				
E	7	12.0	1	.35
L	—	—	—	—
Centropomidae				
E	—	—	—	—
L	1	.5	—	.02
Centropomus sp.				
E	24	10.1	6	.19
L	6	3.26	1	.08
Centropomus undecimalis				
E	—	—	—	—
L	4	2.5	3	.06
Gerreidae				
E	—	—	—	—
L	1	.23	1	.009

FISH (CONTINUED)

Taxa Period	#	Wgt. (g)	MNI	Biomass (kg)
Gobiomorus dormitor				
E	25	8.7	8	.17
L	8	3.2	2	.08
Haemulon sp.				
E	1	.3	1	.01
L	—	—	—	—
Lutjanus sp.				
E	2	2.6	2	.06
L	6	1.38	1	.04
Megalops atlanticus				
E	1	1.1	1	.03
L	10	2.6	1	.06
Mugil sp.				
E	11	4.1	5	.09
L	5	2.29	3	.05
Mycteroperca sp.				
E	—	—	—	—
L	1	.23	1	.009
Pomacanthidae				
E	—	—	—	—
L	1	.2	—	.009
Sciaenidae				
E	1	.1	—	.007
L	—	—	—	—
Serranidae				
E	2	3.5	—	.08
L	3	.46	—	.02
Sparidae				
E	1	.8	—	.02
L	—	—	—	—
Osteichthyes				
E	178	42.0	—	.61
L	161	53.4	—	.74

INVERTEBRATE FAUNA

Taxa Period	#	Wgt. (g)	MNI
Anomalocardia brasiliana			
E	76	40.5	29
L	—	—	—
Arcidae			
E	1	1.5	—
L	—	—	—
Balanus sp.			
E	1	.18	1
L	—	—	—
Bivalvia			
E	195	53.37	—
L	5	1.0	—
Brachidontes exustus			
E	1	.3	1
L	—	—	—
Brachyura			
E	12	1.95	2
L	9	6.9	1
Cardisoma sp.			
E	4	6.1	1
L	4	4.3	2
Chama sp.			
E	1	2.1	1
L	—	—	—
Chione cancellata			
E	9	14.1	3
L	—	—	—
Cittarium pica			
E	1	158.2	1
L	—	—	—
Codakia costata			
E	6	3.2	1
L	—	—	—
Codakia orbicularis			
E	13	9.6	2
L	—	—	—

INVERTEBRATE FAUNA (CONTINUED)

Taxa Period	#	Wgt. (g)	MNI
Crassostrea virginica			
E	145	231	12
L	—	—	—
Crustacea			
E	9	.7	—
L	3	.9	—
Decopoda			
E	75	20.17	—
L	5	.7	—
Donax denticulata			
E	1	.7	1
L	—	—	—
Gastropoda			
E	5	12.4	—
L	1	.8	—
Gecarcinidae			
E	8	3.1	—
L	—	—	—
Isognomon alatus			
E	61	26.05	3
L	—	—	—
Lucina pectinata			
E	13	23	3
L	—	—	—
Mollusca			
E	79	28.1	—
L	5	9.02	—
Mytilidae			
E	1	.1	—
L	—	—	—
Mytilopsis cf. leucopheta			
E	1	.5	—
L	—	—	—
Neritina virginica			
E	2	.7	2
L	—	—	—

INVERTEBRATE FAUNA (CONTINUED)

Taxa Period	#	Wgt. (g)	MNI
Ostreidae			
E	—	—	—
L	3	3.68	—
Strombus gigas			
E	—	—	—
L	1	1,243.2	1
Strombus sp.			
E	4	114.4	1
L	—	—	—
Tellina fausta			
E	1	1.4	1
L	—	—	—

Bibliography

Adams, Edgar H. (arranger)
   1974   *The Julius Guttag Collection of Latin American Coins.* Quarterman Publications, Inc., Lawrence, Mass.
Aga-Oglu, Kamer
   1956   Late Ming and Early Ch'ing Porcelain Fragments from Archaeological Sites in Florida. *Florida Anthropologist* 8:90–110.
Andrews, Kenneth
   1978   *The Spanish Caribbean Trade and Plunder, 1530–1630.* Yale University Press, New Haven.
Arnold, J. Barto, and Robert Weddle
   1978   *The Nautical Archaeology of Padre Island.* Academic Press, New York.
Barber, Edwin Atlee
   1917   *Spanish Glass—In the Collection of the Hispanic Society of America.* G. P. Putnam's Sons, New York.
Barth, Frederick
   1969   *Ethnic Groups and Boundaries.* Little, Brown, Boston.
Bethell, Leslie (editor)
   1984   *The Cambridge History of Latin America.* 2 vols. Cambridge University Press, Cambridge, Eng.
Binford, Lewis R.
   1972   *An Archaeological Perspective.* Seminar Press, New York.
   1981   *Bones: Ancient Men and Modern Myths.* Academic Press, New York.

Boone, James
1984   Majolica Escudillas of the 15th and 16th Centuries: A Typological Analysis of 55 examples from Qsar Es-Seghir. *Historical Archaeology* 18:76–86.

Borah, Woodrow
1984   Trends in Recent Studies of Colonial Latin American Cities, *Hispanic American Historical Review* 64(3):535–54.

Bourne, Edward
1904   *Spain in America.* Benjamin Keene, New York.

Bowser, Frederick
1984   Africans in Spanish American Colonial Society. In *The Cambridge History of Latin America,* vol. 2, edited by Leslie Bethell, pp. 357–79. Cambridge University Press, Cambridge.

Boyd-Bowman, Peter
1976   Patterns of Spanish Emigration to the Indies until 1600. *Hispanic American Historical Review* 56:580–604.

Braudel, Fernand
1967   *Capitalism and Material Life, 1400–1800.* Harper Colophon Books, New York.
1981   *The Structures of Everyday Life, Vol. 1, Civilization and Capitalism, 15th–18th Century.* Harper & Row, New York.

Brown, Ian W.
1977   Historic Trade Bells. *Conference on Historic Site Archaeology Papers* 10:69–82.
1979   Bells. In *Tunica Treasure,* by Jeffrey Brain, pp. 197–205. Papers of the Peabody Museum of Archaeology and Anthropology, No. 71. Harvard University, Cambridge, Mass.

Brown, Vera L.
1928   Contraband Trade As a Factor in the Decline of Spain's Empire in America. *Hispanic American Historical Review* 8:178–189.

Casteel, Richard W.
1972   Some Biases in the Recovery of Archaeological Faunal Remains. *Proceedings of the Prehistoric Society* 36:382–88.
1976   *Fish Remains in Archaeology and Paleo-environmental Studies.* Academic Press, New York.

Chaplin, R. E.
1971   *The Study of Animal Bones from Archaeological Sites.* Seminar Press, New York.

Chaunu, Huguette, and Pierre Chaunu
1959   *Seville et l'Atlantique (1504–1560).* Librairie Armand Colin, Paris.

Council, R. Bruce
  1975   *Archaeology at the Convento de San Francisco.* Master's thesis, Department of Anthropology University of Florida, Gainesville.
Crane, Frederick
  1972   *Extant Medieval Musical Instruments: A Provisional Catalogue by Types.* University of Iowa Press, Iowa City.
Crosby, Alfred W.
  1972   *The Columbian Exchange: Biological and Cultural Consequences of 1492.* Greenwood, Westport, Conn.
Crouch, Dora, D. Garr, and A. Mundigo
  1982   *Spanish City Planning in North America.* Massachusetts Institute of Technology Press, Cambridge.
Cumbaa, Steven
  1975   *Patterns of Resource Use and Cross-cultural Dietary Change in the Spanish Colonial Period.* Ph.D. dissertation, Department of Anthropology, University of Florida, Gainesville. University Microfilms, Ann Arbor.
Deagan, Kathleen A.
  1973   Mestizaje in colonial St. Augustine. *Ethnohistory* 20:55–65.
  1974   *Sex, Status, and Role in the Mestizaje of Spanish Colonial Florida.* Ph.D. dissertation, Department of Anthropology, University of Florida, Gainesville. University Microfilms, Ann Arbor.
  1976   *Archaeology at the National Greek Orthodox Shrine, St. Augustine, Florida.* University of Florida Presses, Gainesville.
  1978   The Material Assemblage of 16th-Century Spanish Florida. *Historical Archaeology* 12:25–50.
  1981   Spanish Colonial Archaeology in the Southeast and the Caribbean, Ms on file, Florida State Museum, Gainesville.
  1983   *Spanish St. Augustine: The Archaeology of a Colonial Creole Community.* Academic Press, New York.
  1986   Initial Encounters: Arawak Responses to European Contact at En Bas Saline, Haiti. Paper presented at the 1st Annual San Salvador Conference, San Salvador, Bahamas.
  1987   *Artifacts of the Spanish Colonies of Florida and the Caribbean, 1500–1800, Vol. 1, Ceramics, Glassware, and Beads.* Smithsonian Press, Washington, D.C.
Defourneaux, Marcelin
  1979   *Daily Life in Spain in the Golden Age,* Stanford University Press, Stanford, Calif.
Eberlein, Harold D.
  1925   *Spanish Interiors, Furniture, and Detail.* Architectural Book Publishing Company, New York.

Elliott, John
   1963   *Imperial Spain, 1479–1716.* Edward Arnold, Ltd., London.
   1984   The Spanish Conquest and Settlement of America. In *The Cambridge History of Latin America,* vol. 1, edited by Leslie Bethell, pp. 149–206. Cambridge University Press, Cambridge.
Ewen, Charles R.
   1985   Cassava and Its Role in the Diet of the West Indies. Paper Presented at the annual meeting of the Florida Academy of Sciences.
Fairbanks, Charles
   1962   A Colono-Indian Ware Milk Pitcher. *Florida Anthropologist* 15:103–06.
   1966   A Feldspar-Inlaid Ceramic Type from Spanish Colonial Sites. *American Antiquity* 31:430–31.
   1973   The Cultural Significance of Spanish Ceramics. In *Ceramics in America,* edited by Ian Quimby, pp. 141–74. University of Virginia Press, Charlottesville.
   1975   Backyard Archaeology as a Research Strategy. *The Conference on Historic Sites Archaeology Papers* 11:133–39.
   1984   The Plantation Archaeology of the Southeastern Coast. *Historical Archaeology* 18(1):1–14.
Fairbanks, Charles, Rochelle Marrinan, Gary Shapiro, Bonnie McEwan, and Alicia Kemper
   1981   Collected Papers from the Puerto Real Project, 1981 Season. Ms. on file, Florida State Museum, Gainesville.
Ferguson, Leland
   1978   Looking for the "Afro" in Colono-Indian Pottery. *The Conference on Historic Sites Archaeology Papers* 12:68–86.
Ffoulkes, Charles
   1967   *The Armourer and His Craft: From the XIth to the XVIth Century.* Benjamin Blom, New York.
Floyd, Troy
   1973   *The Columbus Dynasty in the Caribbean, 1492–1526,* University of New Mexico Press, Albuquerque.
Foster, George
   1960   *Culture and Conquest.* Quadrangle Books, Chicago.
Gibson, Charles
   1966   *Spain in America.* Harper & Row, New York.
Gilbert, B. Miles
   1980   *Mammalian Osteology.* B. Miles Gilbert, Laramie, Wyo.
Gilbert, B. Miles, L. D. Martin, and H. Savage
   1981   *Avian Osteology.* B. Miles Gilbert, Laramie.

Goggin, John
  1960 *The Spanish Olive Jar: An Introductory Study.* Yale University
         Publications in Anthropology, No. 62. Yale University Press, New
         Haven.
  1968 *Spanish Majolica in the New World.* Yale University Publications
         in Anthropology, No. 72. Yale University Press, New Haven.
Gongora, Mario
  1975 *Studies in the Colonial History of Spanish America.* Translated
         by Richard Southern. Cambridge University Press, Cambridge.
Grayson, D. K.
  1984 *Quantitative Zooarchaeology: Topics in the Analysis of Archae-
         ological Faunas.* Academic Press, New York.
Grigson, Caroline
  1976 *A Blueprint for Animal Bone Reports in Archaeology.* Paper pre-
         sented to the International Council for Archaeozoology.
Hamilton, Jennifer
  1982 *Project Puerto Real: A Study of Early Urban Design on His-
         paniola, 1979–1981—Transect Topographic Survey 1982.* Ms. on
         file, Florida State Museum, Gainesville, Florida.
Hamilton, Jennifer, and William Hodges
  1982 *Bayaha: A Preliminary Report.* Ms. on file, Musee de Guahaba,
         Limbe, Haiti.
Haring, C. H.
  1947 *The Spanish Empire in America.* Harcourt Brace Jovanovich,
         New York.
Harrington, J. C., Albert Manucy, and John Goggin
  1955 Archaeological Excavations in the Courtyard of the Castillo de
         San Marcos, St. Augustine, Florida. *Florida Historical Quarterly*
         34(2):101–41.
Helms, Mary W.
  1984 The Indians of the Caribbean and Circum-Caribbean at the End
         of the 15th century. In *The Cambridge History of Latin America,* vol.
         1, edited by Leslie Bethell, pp. 37–57. Cambridge University Press,
         Cambridge.
Hempel, Carl G.
  1965 *Aspects of Scientific Explanation.* Free Press, New York.
Hodges, William
  1979 *How We Found Puerto Real.* Ms. on file, Musee de Guahaba,
         Limbe, Haiti.
  1980 *Puerto Real Sources.* Ms. on file, Musee de Guahaba, Limbe,
         Haiti.

Hoebel, E. Adamson
1972 *Anthropology; The Study of Man.* McGraw-Hill, New York.
Hoffman, Paul E.
1980 *The Spanish Crown and the Defense of the Indies.* Louisiana State University Press, Baton Rouge.
James, Stephen
1985 *The Analysis of the Conde de Tolosa and the Nuestra Señora de Guadalupe Olive Jar Assemblage.* Master's thesis, Department of Anthropology, Texas A&M University, College Station.
Judge, Joseph, and James L. Stanfield
1986 The Islands of Landfall. *National Geographic* 170(5):566–71.
Keen, Benjamin
1969 The Black Legend Revisited: Assumptions and Realities. *Hispanic American Historical Review* 49:703–19.
Knight, Franklin W.
1978 *Patterns Of Colonial Society and Culture: Latin America and the Caribbean, 1492–1804.* Charleston.
Lang, J.
1975 *Conquest and Commerce: Spain and England in the Americas.* Academic Press, New York.
Lavrin, Asuncion
1984 Women in Spanish American Colonial Society. In *The Cambridge History Of Latin America,* vol. 2, edited by Leslie Bethell, pp. 322–55. Cambridge University Press, Cambridge.
Lister, Florence, and Robert Lister
1974 Maiolica in Colonial Spanish America. *Historical Archaeology* 8:17–52.
1976a *A Descriptive Dictionary for 500 Years of Spanish Tradition Ceramics, 13th through 15th Centuries.* Society for Historical Archaeology, Special Publication 1.
1976b Italian Presence in Tin Glazed Ceramics of Spanish America. *Historical Archaeology* 10:28–41.
1978 The First Mexican Maiolicas: Imported and Locally Produced. *Historical Archaeology,* 12:1–24.
1982 *Sixteenth Century Maiolica Pottery in the Valley of Mexico.* Anthropological Papers of the University of Arizona, No. 3. University of Arizona Press, Tucson.
1984 The Potter's Quarter of Colonial Puebla, Mexico. *Historical Archaeology* 18(1):87–102.
Lockhart, James
1969 Encomienda and Hacienda: The Evolution of the Great Estate in

the Spanish Indies. *Hispanic American Historical Review* 49:411–29.
1984 Social Organization and Social Change in Colonial Spanish America. In *The Cambridge History of Latin America,* vol. 2, edited by Leslie Bethell, pp. 265–319. Cambridge University Press, Cambridge.

Lockhart, James, and Stuart Schwartz
1983 *Early Latin America: A History of Colonial Spanish America and Brazil.* Cambridge University Press, Cambridge.

Long, George Ashley
1967 *Archaeological Investigations at Panama Vieja.* Master's thesis, Department of Anthropology, University of Florida, Gainesville.

Lynch, John
1984 *Spain under the Hapsburgs,* vol. 1, 2d ed. New York University Press, New York.

Lyon, Eugene
1981 Research on a Spanish Town on the North Coast of Hispaniola. Ms. on file, Florida State Museum, Gainesville.

Macleod, Murdo J.
1984 Spain and America: The Atlantic Trade, 1492–1972. In *The Cambridge History of Latin America,* vol. 2, edited by Leslie Bethell, pp. 341–88. Cambridge University Press, Cambridge.

Manucy, Albert
1978 *The Houses of St. Augustine.* St. Augustine Historical Society, St. Augustine.

Mariejol, Jean
1961 *The Spain of Ferdinand and Isabella.* Harper & Row, New Brunswick, N.J.

Marrinan, Rochelle
1982 Test Excavations at Building B (Area 2) Puerto Real, Haiti. Project report on file, Florida State Museum, Gainesville.
1986 Acculturation in the Mission Setting: Spanish Florida, 1565–1704. Paper presented at the 43rd Annual Meeting of the Southeastern Archaeological Conference, Nashville.

McAlister, Lyle
1963 Social Structure and Social Change in New Spain. *Hispanic American Historical Review* 43:349–70.
1984 *Spain and Portugal in the New World, 1492–1700.* University of Minnesota Press, Minneapolis.

McEwan, Bonnie
1983 *Spanish Colonial Adaptation on Hispaniola: The Archaeology of Area 35, Puerto Real, Haiti.* Master's thesis, Department of An-

thropology, University of Florida, Gainesville.

Mitchem, Jeffrey M., and Bonnie G. McEwan
 1988 New Data on Early Bells from Florida. *Southeastern Archaeology* 7(1):39–49.

Morison, Samuel E.
 1942 *Admiral of the Ocean Sea: A Life of Christopher Columbus*. Little, Brown, Boston.
 1974 *The European Discovery of America: The Southern Voyages, AD. 1492–1616*. Oxford University Press, Oxford.

Morner, Magnus
 1967 *Race Mixture in the History of Latin America*. Little, Brown, Boston.
 1983 Economic Factors and Stratification in Colonial Spanish America with Special Regard to Elites. *Hispanic American Historical Review* 63:335–69.

Muller, Priscilla E.
 1972 *Jewels in Spain, 1500–1800*. Hispanic Society of America, New York.

Nesmith, Robert
 1955 *The Coinage of the First Mint of the Americas at Mexico City, 1536–1572*. Numismatic Notes and Monographs, No. 31. American Numismatic Society, New York.

Noel-Hume, Ivor
 1978 *A Guide to Artifacts of Colonial America*. Alfred A. Knopf, New York.

Olsen, Stanley J.
 1964 *Mammal Remains from Archaeological Sites*. Papers of the Peabody Museum of Archaeology and Ethnology, Vol. 56, No. 1. Cambridge, Mass.
 1968 *Fish, Amphibian, and Reptile Remains from Archaeological Sites*. Papers of the Peabody Museum of Archaeology and Ethnology, Vol. 56, No. 2. Cambridge, Mass.
 1971 *Zooarchaeology: Animal Bones in Archaeology and Their Interpretation*. Addison-Wesley Modular Publications. Module 2. Reading, Mass.

Oviedo y Valdes, Gonzalo Fernandez de
 1959 *Natural History of the West Indies*. Reprinted, University of North Carolina Press, Chapel Hill. Translated and edited by Sterling A. Stoudemire. Originally published 1527.

Parry, John
 1963 *The Age of Reconnaissance: Discovery and Settlement, 1450 to*

1650. Mentor Books, New York.

1978   *The Spanish Theory of Empire in the 16th Century*. Originally published 1940. Mentor Books, New York.

Parry, John, and Phillip Sherlock

1971   *A Short History of the West Indies*. 3d ed. St. Martin's Press, New York.

Penney, Clara L.

1967   *An Album of Selected Bookbindings*. Hispanic Society of America, New York.

Pike, Ruth

1972   *Aristocrats and Traders: Sevillian Society in the 16th Century*. Cornell University Press, Ithaca, N.Y.

Radisch, William H.

1986   Classification and Interpretation of Stars from Santa Elena: Some Problems and Potential Solutions. Ms. in possession of author.

Redfield, Robert, Melville Herskovits, and Ralph Linton

1936   Memorandum on the Study of Acculturation. *American Anthropologist* 38:149–52.

Reitz, Elizabeth J.

1979   *Spanish and British Subsistence Strategies at St. Augustine, Florida, and Frederica, Georgia*. Ph.D. dissertation, Department of Anthropology, University of Florida, Gainesville. University Microfilms, Ann Arbor.

1982   *Analysis of Vertebrate Fauna from Area 19, Puerto Real, Haiti*. Project report on file, Florida State Museum, Gainesville.

1986   Vertebrate Fauna from Locus 39, Puerto Real, Haiti. *Journal of Field Archaeology* 13:317–28.

Reitz, Elizabeth J., and Dan Cordier

1983   Use of Allometry in Zooarchaeological Analysis. In *Animals And Archaeology: Shell Middens, Fishes, and Birds*, edited by J. Clatton-Brock and C. Grigson, pp. 237–52. BAR International Series 183, London.

Reitz, Elizabeth J., and Stephen L. Cumbaa

1983   Diet and Foodways of Eighteenth-Century Spanish St. Augustine. In *Spanish St. Augustine: The Archaeology of a Colonial Creole Community*, edited by Kathleen Deagan, pp. 151–86. Academic Press, New York.

Reitz, Elizabeth J., and Margaret Scarry

1985   *Reconstructing Historic Subsistence with an Example from Sixteenth-Century Spanish Florida*. Special Publication Series No. 3. Society for Historical Archaeology, Glassboro, N.J.

Rouse, Irving
  1948   The Arawak. In *Handbook of South American Indians,* edited by Julian Steward, vol. 4, pp. 507–46. Bureau of American Ethnology, Bulletin 143, Smithsonian Institution, Washington D.C.
  1986   *Migrations in Prehistory.* Yale University Press, New Haven.
Sauer, Carl O.
  1966   *The Early Spanish Main.* University of California Press, Berkeley.
Schiffer, Michael B.
  1972   Archaeological Context and Systemic Context. *American Antiquity* 37:156–65.
Shapiro, Gary
  1984   A Soil Resistivity Survey of 16th-Century Puerto Real, Haiti. *Journal of Field Archaeology* 11:101–09.
Simpson, Lesley B.
  1966   *The Encomienda in New Spain.* University of California Press, Berkeley.
Skowronek, Russell
  1987   Ceramics and Commerce: The 1554 *Flota* Revisited. Paper presented at the Annual Meeting of the Society of Historical Archaeology, Savannah.
Smith, Greg C.
  1986   *Non-European Pottery at the Sixteenth Century Spanish Site of Puerto Real, Haiti.* Master's thesis, Department of Anthropology, University of Florida, Gainesville.
Smith, Hale G.
  1962   *El Morro.* Notes in Anthropology, Vol. 6. Florida State University, Tallahassee.
Smith, Marvin T., and Mary E. Good
  1982   *Early Sixteenth Century Beads in the Spanish Colonial Trade.* Cottonlandia Museum Publications, Greenwood, Mich.
South, Stanley
  1977   *Method and Theory in Historical Archaeology.* Academic Press, New York.
Spicer, Edward H. (editor)
  1961   *Perspectives in American Indian Culture Change.* University of Chicago Press, Chicago.
Spicer, Edward H.
  1962   *Cycles of Conquest: The Impact of Spain, Mexico, and the United States on the Indians of the Southwest, 1533–1960.* University of Arizona Press, Tucson.
Stahl, P. W.
  1982   On Small Mammal Remains in Archaeological Context. *Amer-*

ican Antiquity 47:267–70.

Stein, Stanley, and Barbara Stein
1970 *The Colonial Heritage of Latin America.* Oxford University Press, New York.

Steward, Julian
1943 Acculturation Studies in Latin America: Some Needs and Problems. *American Anthropologist* 45:198–204.

Todorov, Tzvetan
1984 *The Conquest of America.* Translated by Richard Howard. Harper Colophon Books, New York.

Verlinden, Charles
1953 Italian Influence in Iberian Colonization. *Hispanic American Historical Review* 33:199–211.

Vernon, Richard
1988 17th Century Apalachee Colono-Ware as a Reflection of Demography, Economics, and Acculturation. *Historical Archaeology* 22:76–82.

Vicens Vives, Jaime
1967 *Approaches to the History of Spain.* University of California Press, Berkeley.
1969 *An Economic History of Spain.* Princeton University Press, Princeton, N.J.

Williams, Maurice
1986 Sub-surface Patterning at Puerto Real: A Sixteenth-Century Spanish Town on Haiti's North Coast. *Journal of Field Archaeology* 13:283–96.

Willis, Raymond
1976 *The Archaeology of 16th Century Nueva Cadiz.* Master's thesis, Department of Anthropology, University of Florida, Gainesville.
1981 Current Research at Puerto Real. *Society for Historical Archaeology Newsletter* 14(2):5.
1984 *Empire and Architecture at 16th Century Puerto Real, Hispaniola: An Archaeological Perspective.* Ph.D. dissertation, Department of Anthropology, University of Florida, Gainesville. University Microfilms, Ann Arbor.

Wing, Elizabeth and Antoinette Brown
1979 *Paleonutrition: Method and Theory in Prehistoric Foodways.* Academic Press, New York.

Woods, Charles A.
1980 Collecting Fossil Mammals in the Greater Antilles: An Immense Journey. *The Plaster Jacket.* Florida State Museum, Gainesville.

Wright, Irene
    1939   Rescates: With Special Reference to Cuba, 1599–1610. *The Hispanic American Historical Review* 19:56–72.
Zendegui, Guillermo
    1977   City Planning in the Spanish Colonies. *Americas,* Special Supplement. February 1977.
Ziegler, Alan
    1973   *Inference from Prehistoric Faunal Remains.* Addison-Wesley Module in Anthropology, No. 43. Addison-Wesley, New York.

Index